YOUR CRIMINAL JUSTICE CAREER

DATE DUE

DATE DUE	
FEB 2 9 2000	
SEP 2 0 2001	
JUL 1 1 2005	
OCT 0 2 2007	
NOV 0 4 2008	
AUG 1 3 2015	
JUN 2 9 2017	

BRODART.   Cat. No. 23-221

YOUR CRIMINAL JUSTICE CAREER

A Guidebook

The Justice Research Association

(with information from the Bureau of Labor Statistics)

Compiled by Frank Schmalleger

Prentice Hall, Upper Saddle River, New Jersey 07458

Library of Congress Cataloging-in-Publication Data

Your criminal justice career : a guidebook / the Justice Research
   Association.
      p.   cm.
   ISBN 0-13-085204-X
   1. Criminal justice, Administration of—Vocational guidance—
United States.   I. Justice Research Association.
HV9950.Y68   2000
364'.023'73—dc21   99-30352
                                                                     CIP

Publisher: *Dave Garza*
Acquisitions Editor: *Neil Marquardt*
Managing Editor: *Mary Carnis*
Production Management: *Jill Lynch at North Market Street Graphics*
Production Editor: *M. R. Carey at North Market Street Graphics*
Production Liaison: *Adele M. Kupchik*
Director of Manufacturing and Production: *Bruce Johnson*
Manufacturing Buyer: *Ed O'Dougherty*
Creative Director: *Marianne Frasco*
Senior Design Coordinator: *Miguel Ortiz*
Art Director: *Jayne Conte*
Cover Designer: *Joe Sengotta*
Associate Art Director: *Marianne Frasco*
Typesetting: *North Market Street Graphics*
Marketing Manager: *Shannon Simonsen*
Marketing Assistant: *Adam Kloza*
Printer/Binder: *R. R. Donnelley & Sons, Co., Harrisonburg*

Printed in the United States of America

10 9 8 7 6 5 4 3 2 1

ISBN 0-13-085204-X

Prentice-Hall International (UK) Limited, *London*
Prentice-Hall of Australia Pty. Limited, *Sydney*
Prentice-Hall Canada Inc., *Toronto*
Prentice-Hall Hispanoamericana, S.A., *Mexico*
Prentice-Hall of India Private Limited, *New Delhi*
Prentice-Hall of Japan, Inc., *Tokyo*
Pearson Education Asia Pte. Ltd., *Singapore*
Editora Prentice-Hall do Brasil, Ltda., *Rio de Janeiro*

Contents

Foreword

According to a recent *New York Times* article,[1] the criminal justice field is undergoing explosive growth. The *Times* estimated that in 1998 there were more than 350,000 undergraduate students majoring in criminal justice at the graduate and undergraduate levels in the United States. Add to that the thousands of other students who take criminal justice courses out of curiosity or to fulfill an elective requirement, and the number of students enrolled in such courses in a given year is nothing short of phenomenal.

One reason for the large and rapidly growing cadre of criminal justice majors is a fascination with criminals, and with understanding criminal behavior. Popular movies and television shows have piqued the interest of many, leading to a flood of students into criminal justice curricula. But at another level, says the *Times*, "the flood of new courses and students is a reflection of the intellectual success of criminal justice." Many now entering the justice field are led by personal idealism—and hope to make a difference in the fight against crime, and in addressing the conditions which give rise to unlawful behavior.

Fortunately for students in the field, the criminal justice system in this country is growing rapidly—and the job market for criminal justice personnel appears able to accommodate most graduating students for years to come.

This guide hopes to meet the needs of criminal justice students who will soon be entering the job market. It brings

[1]Fox Butterfield, "A Newcomer Breaks Into the Liberal Arts: Criminal Justice," *New York Times*, December 5, 1998, p. B1.

together, in one convenient place, information from the U.S. Bureau of Labor Statistics (BLS) on criminal justice and public safety occupations. Most of the information contained in this volume comes from the BLS's 1998–1999 *Occupational Outlook Handbook.* It has been adapted here (as well as occasionally reworded) to assist college and university criminal justice students preparing for careers in the justice and public safety fields.

The BLS *Occupational Outlook Handbook* is a massive publication, covering employment projections for the nation in great detail, and describing a large number of career areas. Sorting through the *Handbook*—which contains more than a thousand employment categories—and finding material of interest can be a daunting task. Hence, it is our hope that this guide will make important BLS information on criminal justice careers easily and readily available to those interested in working in the American justice system and in public safety occupations.

Much of the information contained in this guide is also available at the federal government's *Occupational Outlook Handbook* site on the World Wide Web at http://stats.bls.gov/ocohome.htm and at "Dr. Frank Schmalleger's Cybrary of Criminal Justice Links," http://talkjustice.com/files/cybrary.htm.

Portions of Chapter 12 come from the Criminal Justice Distance Learning Consortium's (CJDLC's) *Definitive Guide to Criminal Justice and Criminology on the World Wide Web* (Prentice Hall, 1999). CJDLC is a project of the Justice Research Association, and we are grateful to them for making this information available for use here.

Thank you for using this guide. If you have any comments or suggestions, please e-mail me at justice@hargray.com.

Frank Schmalleger, Ph.D., Director
The Justice Research Association

CHAPTER 1

Finding a Job

$\mathcal{S}$ignificant Points

- Choice of employment is one of the most crucial decisions anyone can make.
- Some of the best jobs information is readily available through personal contacts, classified advertisements, public libraries, the World Wide Web, and other easily accessible sources.

*I*ntroduction

Finding employment (and accepting a job offer) is one of the most crucial decisions you can make. Your choice of careers

The material in this chapter is adapted from Bureau of Labor Statistics, 1998–1999 *Occupational Outlook Handbook*.

is an important determinant of life satisfaction. A job can be rewarding in a number of ways—from the daily personal satisfaction that comes from helping others, or from knowing that you are contributing positively to society, to the financial rewards that arrive every month in the form of a paycheck. The reward of knowing that you are helping others is commonly cited by those entering criminal justice and public safety occupations as one reason for their choice of careers.

Salary, of course, is also an important job consideration. But when choosing a job, it is good to keep in mind that the financial benefits of employment extend beyond salary to encompass fringe benefits—including health and retirement plans paid for or sponsored by employers. Such benefits can have a significant impact on the quality of life, especially if you or a family member become sick, or as retirement time approaches.

For college students, job seeking usually begins in the months immediately prior to graduation. Career experts tell us, however, that the more time you spend considering what kind of job you want, the more likely you are to find satisfying employment.

What are some of the best sources of information that you can use in finding and choosing a job? According to the 1998–1999 *Occupational Outlook Handbook*, they include the following:

PERSONAL CONTACTS

Your network of family, friends, and acquaintances may offer one of the most effective ways to find a job. They may help you directly or put you in touch with someone else who can. Such networking can lead to meeting with someone who is hiring for an agency or firm or who knows of specific job openings.

The people close to you—your family and friends—can be extremely helpful in providing career information. They may be able to answer your questions or put you in touch with someone who can. This type of networking can lead to meeting someone who can answer your questions about a specific

career, agency, or company, and who can provide inside information and other helpful hints. This is an effective way to learn what type of training is necessary for a certain position and how someone in that position entered the field, the prospects for advancement, and what they like and dislike about the work.

CLASSIFIED ADS

The "Help Wanted" ads in newspapers list hundreds of jobs. You should realize, however, that many other job openings are not listed, and that the classified ads sometimes do not give all the important information. Many offer little or no description of the job, working conditions, or pay. Some ads do not identify the employer. They may simply give a post office box for sending your resume. This makes follow-up inquiries very difficult. Furthermore, some ads offer out-of-town jobs; others advertise employment agencies rather than actual employment openings.

Keep the following in mind when using classified ads:

1. Do not rely solely on the classifieds to find a job; follow other leads as well.
2. Answer ads promptly, since openings may be filled quickly, even before the ad stops appearing in the paper.
3. Read the ads every day, particularly the Sunday edition, which usually includes the most listings.
4. Beware of "no experience necessary" ads. These ads often signal low wages, poor working conditions, or commission work.
5. Keep a record of all ads to which you have responded, including the specific skills, educational background, and personal qualifications required for each position.

INTERNET NETWORKS AND RESOURCES

A variety of information is available on the Internet, including jobs and job search resources and techniques. The growth of

online listings has made available a wide variety of resources at your fingertips—24 hours a day, 7 days a week. Many companies, professional societies, academic institutions, and government agencies maintain online resources or homepages with the latest information on their organizations and their activities.

Listings may include information such as government documents, schedules of events, job openings, and even networking contacts. Listings for academic institutions often provide links to career counseling and placement services through career resource centers, as well as information on financing your education. Colleges and universities also offer online guides to campus facilities and admission requirements and procedures.

The variety of career information available through the Internet provides much of the same information available through libraries, career centers, and guidance offices. However, no single network or resource will contain all desired information, so be prepared to search a variety of different places. As in a library search, look through various lists by field or discipline, or by using particular keywords.

When searching employment databases on the Internet, it is sometimes possible to post your resume online or send it to an employer via e-mail. Some sources provide this service free of charge; however, be careful that you are not going to incur any additional charges for postings or updates. A good place to start your job search is *America's Job Bank*. It can be found at www.ajb.dni.us/index.html.

PUBLIC EMPLOYMENT SERVICES

The state employment service, sometimes called the Job Service, operates in coordination with the U.S. Employment Service of the U.S. Department of Labor. About 1,700 local offices help jobseekers find jobs and help employers find qualified workers at no cost to themselves. To find the office nearest you, look in the state government telephone listings under "Job Service" or "Employment."

PUBLIC LIBRARIES, CAREER CENTERS, AND GUIDANCE OFFICES

These institutions maintain a great deal of up-to-date career material. To begin your library search, look at the computer listings under "Vocations" or "Careers" and then under specific fields. Check the periodicals section, where you will find trade and professional magazines and journals about specific occupations and industries. Familiarize yourself with the concerns and activities of potential employers by skimming their annual reports and other information they distribute to the public. You can also find occupational information on video cassettes, in kits, and through computerized information systems. Don't forget the librarians; they can be a great source of information and can save you time by directing you to the information you need.

Check your school's career centers for programs such as individual counseling and testing, guest speakers, field trips, and career days. Also, read through any pamphlets that describe employment.

Always assess career guidance materials carefully. Information should be current. Beware of materials that seem to glamorize the occupation, overstate the earnings, or exaggerate the demand for workers.

COUNSELORS

You may wish to seek help from a counselor. These professionals are trained to help you discover your strengths and weaknesses, guide you through an evaluation of your goals and values, and help you determine what you want in a career. The counselor will not tell you what to do, but will administer interest inventories and aptitude tests, interpret the results, and help you explore your options. Counselors also may discuss local job markets and the entry requirements and costs of the schools, colleges, or training programs offering preparation for the kind of work that interests you. You can find counselors in the following places:

1. High school guidance offices
2. College career planning and placement offices
3. Placement offices in private vocational/technical schools and institutions
4. Vocational rehabilitation agencies
5. Counseling services offered by community organizations
6. Private counseling agencies and private practices
7. State employment service offices affiliated with the U.S. Employment Service

Before employing the services of a private counselor or agency, you may want to seek recommendations and check their credentials. The International Association of Counseling Services (IACS) accredits counseling services throughout the country. To receive a listing of accredited services for your region, send a self-addressed, stamped, business-size envelope to: IACS, 101 South Whiting St., Suite 211, Alexandria, VA 22304.

The *Directory of Counseling Services,* an IACS publication providing employment counseling and other assistance, may be available in your library or school career counseling center. A list of certified career counselors by state can be obtained from:

The National Board of Certified Counselors
3 Terrace Way, Suite D
Greensboro, NC 27403-3660
Phone: (910) 547-0607

PROFESSIONAL SOCIETIES, TRADE ASSOCIATIONS, LABOR UNIONS, BUSINESS FIRMS, AND EDUCATIONAL INSTITUTIONS

These organizations provide a variety of free or inexpensive career materials. For information on such organizations, consult directories in your library's reference section. You may want to start with *The Guide to American Directories* or *The Directory of Directories.* Another useful resource is *The Ency-*

clopedia of Associations, an annual publication listing trade associations, professional societies, labor unions, and fraternal and patriotic organizations.

The National Technical Information Service Audiovisual Center, a central source for audiovisual material produced by the U.S. Government, sells material on jobs and careers. For a catalog, contact:

NTIS Audiovisual Center
Springfield, VA 22161
Phone: (800) 553-6847

For first-hand experience in an occupation, you may wish to work as an intern. Some internships offer academic credit or pay a stipend, and can lead to a full-time job after graduation. Check with guidance offices, college career resource centers, or directly with employers for opportunities.

JOB MATCHING AND REFERRAL SERVICES

At the state employment service office, an interviewer can determine if you are "job ready" or if counseling and testing services would be helpful first. After you are job ready, you may examine available job listings and select openings that interest you. A staff member can then describe the job openings in detail and arrange for interviews with prospective employers. Employment counselors can arrange for tests to assess your occupational aptitudes and interests. They will also help you choose and prepare for a career.

America's Job Bank, run by the U.S. Department of Labor's Employment and Training Administration, provides information on preparing your resume and using the Internet for your job search, trends in the U.S. job market and state occupational projections, and approximately 500,000 job openings on any given day. A wide range of jobs are listed all over the country, and most are full-time jobs in the private sector. Job seekers can access these listings through the Internet; computers with access to the Internet are available to the public in any local public employment service office,

as well as in schools, libraries, and several hundred military installations.

Tips for Finding the Right Job, a U.S. Department of Labor pamphlet, offers advice on determining your job skills, organizing your job search, writing a resume, and making the most of an interview. *Job Search Guide: Strategies for Professionals,* another U.S. Department of Labor publication, discusses specific steps that job seekers can follow to identify employment opportunities. This publication includes sections on such things as handling job loss, managing personal resources, assessing personal skills and interests, researching the job market, conducting the job search, and networking. Check with your state employment service office, or order a copy of these publications from the U.S. Government Printing Office's Superintendent of Documents. Phone (202) 512-1800 for price and ordering information.

PRIVATE EMPLOYMENT AGENCIES

These agencies can be helpful, but they are in business to make money. Most agencies operate on a commission basis, with the fee dependent upon a percentage of the salary paid to a successful applicant. You or the employer will have to pay a sizable fee. Find out the exact cost and who is responsible for paying it before using the service.

While employment agencies can help you save time and contact employers who otherwise might be difficult to locate, in cases where you are responsible for the fee, your costs may outweigh the benefits. Consider any guarantee they offer when determining the cost.

COLLEGE CAREER PLANNING AND PLACEMENT OFFICES

College placement offices facilitate matching job openings for their students and alumni. They set up appointments and use the facilities for interviews with recruiters. Placement offices usually list part-time, temporary, and summer jobs offered on campus. They also list jobs in regional business, nonprofit, and government organizations. Students can receive career

counseling and testing, job search advice, and use of the career resource library. Here you may attend workshops on such topics as job search strategy, resume writing, letter writing, and effective interviewing; critique drafts of resumes and watch videotapes of mock interviews; explore files of resumes and references; and attend job fairs conducted by the office.

COMMUNITY AGENCIES

Many nonprofit organizations, including churches, synagogues, and vocational rehabilitation agencies, offer counseling, career development, and job placement services, generally targeted to a particular group, such as women, youth, minorities, ex-offenders, or older workers.

EMPLOYERS

It is possible to apply directly to employers without a referral. You may locate a potential employer in the Yellow Pages, in directories of local chambers of commerce, and in other directories that provide information about employers. When you find an employer you are interested in, you can send a cover letter and resume even if you are not certain that an opening exists.

FEDERAL JOB INFORMATION

Information on getting a job with the federal government is available from the Office of Personnel Management through a telephone-based system. Consult your telephone directory under U.S. Government for a local number or call (912) 757-3000 [TDD (912) 744-2299]. Information also is available on the Internet at www.usajobs.opm.gov.

CHAPTER 2

Applying for a Job

Significant Points

- Most jobs require that you complete and submit an application and a resume, along with a cover letter explaining why you are interested in the position and how you qualify for it.
- A cover letter is a way to introduce yourself to employers. It should be carefully written.
- A job interview gives you an excellent opportunity to showcase your qualifications to a potential employer.
- You should carefully prepare for a job interview since it is often the final deciding factor in an employment decision-making process.

The material in this chapter is adapted from Bureau of Labor Statistics, 1998–1999 *Occupational Outlook Handbook*.

Introduction

This chapter discusses resumes, cover letters, application forms, and employment interviews—all of which are important considerations in applying for a job. Although the material covered in this chapter is generic, it is as applicable to jobs in the criminal justice and public safety fields as it is to other types of employment.

Resumes and Application Forms

Resumes and application forms are two ways to provide employers with written evidence of your qualifications and skills. Most information appears on both the resume and the application form, but the way it is presented differs. Some employers prefer a resume, while others require an application form. The following section presents the basic information you should include in your resume.

There are many ways of organizing a resume. Depending on the job, you should choose the format that best highlights your skills, training, and experience. It may be helpful to look in a variety of books and publications in your local library or bookstore for different examples.

Cover Letters

A cover letter is sent with a resume or application form, as a way to introduce yourself to employers. It should capture the employer's attention, should follow a business letter format, and should usually include the following information:

- The name and address of the specific person to whom the letter is addressed

- The reason for your interest in the agency, company, or position
- Your main qualifications for the position (in brief)
- A request for an interview
- Your home and work phone numbers

What Goes into a Resume

- Name, address, and telephone number.
- Employment objective. State the type of work or specific job you are seeking.
- Education, including school name and address, dates of attendance, curriculum, and highest grade completed or degree awarded.
- Experience, paid or volunteer. Include the following for each job: job title, name and location of employer, and dates of employment. Briefly describe your job duties.
- Special skills, proficiency in foreign languages, achievements, membership in organizations, and volunteer work. Note on your resume: "References available upon request."

Interviewing

An interview gives you the opportunity to showcase your qualifications to an employer, so it pays to be well prepared. The information that follows provides some helpful hints.

JOB INTERVIEW TIPS

Preparation
- Learn about the organization.
- Have a specific job or jobs in mind.
- Review your qualifications for the job.

- Prepare answers to broad questions about yourself.
- Review your resume.
- Practice an interview with a friend or relative.
- Arrive before the scheduled time of your interview.

Personal Appearance
- Be well groomed.
- Dress appropriately.
- Do not chew gum or smoke.

The Interview
- Relax and answer each question concisely.
- Respond promptly.
- Use good manners.
- Learn the name of your interviewer and shake hands as you meet.
- Use proper English and avoid slang.
- Be cooperative and enthusiastic.
- Ask questions about the position and the organization.
- Thank the interviewer, and follow up with a letter.

Test (If Employer Gives One)

- Listen closely to instructions.
- Read each question carefully.
- Write legibly and clearly.
- Budget your time wisely and don't dwell on one question.

Information to Bring to an Interview

- *Social Security number.*
- *Driver's license number.*
- *Resume.* Although not all employers require applicants to bring a resume, you should be able to furnish the interviewer information about your education, training, and previous employment.
- *References.* An employer usually requires three references. Get permission from people before using their names, and make sure they will give you a good reference. Try to avoid using relatives.

CHAPTER 3

Evaluating a Job Offer

$\mathcal{S}$ignificant Points

- When you receive a job offer you should evaluate it carefully.
- Knowing what you want and expect from a job will help you decide whether or not to accept the offer.
- Researching potential employers before accepting an offer of employment can help ensure that you will be satisfied after you start working.

/ntroduction

Once you receive a job offer, you are faced with a difficult decision and must evaluate the offer carefully. Fortunately,

The material in this chapter is adapted from Bureau of Labor Statistics, 1998–1999 *Occupational Outlook Handbook*.

most organizations will not expect you to accept or reject an offer immediately.

There are many issues to consider when assessing a job offer. Will the agency or organization be a good place to work? Will the job be interesting? How are opportunities for advancement? Is the salary fair? Does the employer offer good benefits?

If you have not already figured out exactly what you want, the following discussion may help you develop a set of criteria for judging job offers, whether you are starting a career, reentering the labor force after a long absence, or planning a career change. The information presented here is not specific to criminal justice and public safety careers, but is applicable to most professions. Here's are some things you should consider:

THE ORGANIZATION

Background information on an organization can help you decide whether it is a good place for you to work. Factors to consider include the organization's business or activity, financial condition, age, size, and location.

You can generally get background information on an organization, particularly a large organization, by telephoning its public relations office. A public company's annual report to the stockholders tells about its corporate philosophy, history, products or services, goals, and financial status. Most large government agencies, including criminal justice agencies, publish annual reports, and smaller ones can furnish printed materials that describe their programs and missions. Press releases, company and agency newsletters or magazines, and recruitment brochures also can be useful. Ask the agency or organization for any other items that might interest a prospective employee.

If possible, speak to current or former employees of the organization. Background information on the organization also may be available on the Internet or at your public or school library. If you cannot get an annual report, check the

library for reference directories that may provide basic facts about the agency or company, such as its purpose or function, orientation, products, organizational philosophy, and number of employees.

Stories about an agency or organization can often be found in magazines and newspapers, and can tell you a great deal about its successes, failures, and plans for the future. You can identify articles on an agency or company by looking under its name in periodical or computerized indexes such as the following—however, it may not be useful to look back more than two or three years.

Career centers at colleges and universities often have information on employers that is not available in libraries. Ask a career center representative how to find out about a particular organization. The career center may have an entire file of information on the employer.

- *Is the organization's business or activity in keeping with your own interests and beliefs?* It will be easier to apply yourself to the work if you are enthusiastic about what the organization does.
- *How will the size of the organization affect you?* Large organizations generally offer a greater variety of training programs and career paths, more managerial levels for advancement, and better employee benefits than small organizations. Large employers may also have more advanced technologies. However, jobs in large agencies or companies may tend to be highly specialized. Jobs in small agencies or small firms may offer broader authority and responsibility, a closer working relationship with top management, and a chance to clearly see your contribution to the success of the organization.
- *Does it make any difference to you whether the employer is a public agency or a private company?* A privately owned company may be controlled by an individual or a family, which can mean that key jobs are reserved for relatives and friends. A publicly owned company is controlled by a board of directors responsible to the stockholders. A pub-

lic agency, like a law enforcement agency, is similar to a publicly owned company in that key jobs are open to anyone with talent.

THE NATURE OF THE JOB

Even if everything else about the job is good, you will be unhappy if you dislike the day-to-day work. Determining in advance whether you will like the work may be difficult. However, the more you find out about it before accepting or rejecting the job offer, the more likely you are to make the right choice. Actually working in the industry and, if possible, for the agency or company would provide considerable insight. You can gain work experience through part-time, temporary, or summer jobs, or through work-study programs and internships while in school, all of which can lead to permanent job offers.

- *Where is the job located?*   If it is in another section of the country, you need to consider the cost of living, the availability of housing and transportation, and the quality of educational and recreational facilities in the new location. Even if the place of work is in your area, consider the time and expense of commuting in your decision.

- *Does the work match your interests and make good use of your skills?*   The duties and responsibilities of the job should be explained in enough detail to answer this question.

- *Are you comfortable with the hours?*   Most jobs involve regular hours—for example, 40 hours a week, during the day, Monday through Friday. Other jobs, especially those in law enforcement and correctional agencies, require night, weekend, or holiday work. In addition, some jobs routinely require overtime to meet deadlines or sales or production goals, or to better serve customers. Consider the effect of work hours on your personal life.

- *How long do most people who enter this job stay with the agency or company?*   High turnover can mean dissatis-

faction with the nature of the work or something else about the job.

OPPORTUNITIES OFFERED BY EMPLOYERS

A good job offers you opportunities to learn new skills, increase your earnings, and rise to positions of greater authority, responsibility, and prestige. A lack of opportunities can dampen interest in the work and result in frustration and boredom. The company should have a training plan for you. What valuable new skills does the agency or company plan to teach you? The employer should give you some idea of promotion possibilities within the organization. What is the next step on the career ladder? If you have to wait for a job to become vacant before you can be promoted, how long does this usually take? Employers differ on their policies regarding promotion from within the organization. When opportunities for advancement do arise, will you compete with applicants from outside the company? Can you apply for jobs for which you qualify elsewhere within the organization, or is mobility within the organization limited?

SALARIES AND BENEFITS

Wait for the employer to introduce these subjects. Some employers will not talk about pay until they have decided to hire you. In order to know if their offer is reasonable, you need a rough estimate of what the job should pay. You may have to go to several sources for this information. Try to find family, friends, or acquaintances who recently were hired for similar jobs. Ask your teachers and the staff in the college placement office about starting pay for graduates with your qualifications. Help-wanted ads in newspapers sometimes give salary ranges for similar positions.

If you are considering the salary and benefits for a job in another geographic area, make allowances for differences in the cost of living, which may be significantly higher in a large metropolitan area than in a smaller city, town, or rural area.

You also should learn the organization's policy regarding overtime. Depending on the job, you may or may not be exempt from laws requiring the employer to compensate you for overtime. Find out how many hours you will be expected to work each week and whether you will receive overtime pay or compensatory time off for working more than the specified number of hours in a week.

Also take into account that the starting salary is just that, the start. Your salary should be reviewed on a regular basis—many organizations do it every year. How much can you expect to earn after one, two, or three or more years? An employer cannot be specific about the amount of pay if it includes commissions and bonuses.

Benefits can also add a lot to your base pay, but they vary widely. Find out exactly what the benefit package includes and how much of the costs you must bear.

Check the library or your school's career center for salary surveys such as those conducted by the National Association of Colleges and Employers or various professional associations.

Data on wages and benefits are also available from:

Bureau of Labor Statistics
Office of Compensation and Working Conditions
2 Massachusetts Ave. NE, Room 4160
Washington, DC 20212-0001
Phone: (202) 606-6225

Data from the National Compensation Survey, which integrates data from three existing BLS programs—the Employment Cost Index, the Occupational Compensation Survey, and the Employee Benefits Survey—will become available by the year 2000 from the BLS office above and from the Internet: http://stats.bls.gov/comhome.htm

Current Population Survey (CPS) data on median weekly earnings of full-time wage and salary workers, by detailed occupation, are available from:

Bureau of Labor Statistics
Office of Employment and Unemployment Statistics
2 Massachusetts Ave. NE, Room 4945
Washington, DC 20212-0001
Phone: (202) 606-6400

CPS data can also be accessed at the following Internet address: http://stats.bls.gov/cpsaatab.htm.

CHAPTER 4

Working as an Attorney

$\mathcal{S}$ignificant Points

- There are about 622,000 attorneys practicing law in the United States, and another 78,000 judges.
- Formal educational requirements for the practice of law usually include a four-year college degree, followed by three years in law school. After that, all states require applicants for admission to the bar to pass a written bar examination.
- The median annual salary of all lawyers was about $60,000 in 1996, although income varied greatly depending upon the area of law in which an attorney specialized, the nature of the firm for which he or she worked, and the attorney's reputation within the field.

The material in this chapter is adapted from Bureau of Labor Statistics, 1998–1999 *Occupational Outlook Handbook*.

- Competition for admission to many law schools is intense, as the number of applicants greatly exceeds the number that may be admitted.
- Although the job market for lawyers expanded rapidly from 1970 to 1990, opportunities are now more limited. The number of law school graduates is expected to continue to strain the economy's capacity to absorb them.

*N*ature of the Work

LAWYERS

Lawyers, also called *attorneys,* act as both advocates and advisors in our society. As advocates, they represent one of the parties in criminal and civil trials by presenting evidence in court supporting their clients. As advisors, lawyers counsel their clients as to their legal rights and obligations, and suggest particular courses of action in business and personal matters. Whether acting as advocates or advisors, all attorneys interpret the law and apply it to specific situations.

Lawyers research the purposes behind laws and judicial decisions that have been applied to circumstances similar to those faced by their clients. While all lawyers continue to use law libraries to prepare cases, some supplement their search of conventional printed sources with computer sources. Software can be used to search legal literature automatically, and to identify legal texts relevant to a specific case. In litigation involving many supporting documents, lawyers may use computers to organize and index material. Tax lawyers use computers to make tax computations and explore alternative tax strategies for clients.

Lawyers increasingly use the Internet for research and to advertise their services. Ethical standards for advertising on the Internet are still evolving. Lawyers also use electronic filing, videoconferencing, and voice-recognition technology. Electronic filing promotes the sharing of information by providing all parties in a case access to a database with all official filings, briefs, and other court documents; these technologies also save time and reduce legal costs.

Lawyers communicate the information obtained through research to others. They advise clients and draw up legal documents, such as wills and contracts. Lawyers may not disclose matters discussed in confidence with clients. They hold positions of great responsibility, and are obligated to adhere to a strict code of ethics.

The more detailed aspects of a lawyer's job depend upon his or her field of specialization and position. While all lawyers are licensed to represent parties in court, some appear in court more frequently than others; some lawyers specialize in trial work. Their ability to think quickly and speak with ease and authority as well as their familiarity with courtroom rules and strategy are particularly important in trial work. However, trial lawyers still spend most of their time outside the courtroom, conducting research, interviewing clients and witnesses, and handling other details in preparation for trial.

Besides trials, lawyers may specialize in other areas, such as bankruptcy, probate, or international law. Environmental lawyers, for example, may represent public interest groups, waste disposal companies, or construction firms in their dealings with the Environmental Protection Agency (EPA) and other state and federal agencies. They help clients prepare and file for licenses and applications for approval before certain activities may occur. They also represent clients' interests in administrative adjudications.

Some lawyers concentrate in the growing field of intellectual property. These lawyers help protect clients' claims to copyrights, art work under contract, product designs, and computer programs. Still other lawyers advise insurance companies about the legality of insurance transactions. They write insurance policies to conform with the law and to protect companies from unwarranted claims. They review claims filed against insurance companies and represent the companies in court.

The majority of lawyers are in private practice, where they concentrate on criminal or civil law. In criminal law, lawyers represent individuals who have been charged with crimes and

argue their cases in courts of law. In civil law, attorneys assist clients with litigation, wills, trusts, contracts, mortgages, titles, and leases. Others handle only public interest cases—civil or criminal—which may have a potential impact extending well beyond the individual client.

Lawyers are sometimes employed full time by a single client. If the client is a corporation, the lawyer is known as *house counsel,* and usually advises the company concerning legal issues related to its business activities. These issues might involve patents, government regulations, contracts with other companies, property interests, or collective-bargaining agreements with unions.

A significant number of attorneys are employed at the various levels of government. Lawyers who work for state attorneys general, prosecutors, public defenders, and courts play a key role in the criminal justice system. At the federal level, attorneys investigate cases for the Department of Justice or other agencies. Government lawyers also help develop programs, draft and interpret laws and legislation, establish enforcement procedures, and argue civil and criminal cases on behalf of the government.

Other lawyers work for legal aid societies—private, nonprofit organizations established to serve disadvantaged people. These lawyers generally handle civil, rather than criminal, cases.

A relatively small number of trained attorneys work in law schools. Most are faculty members who specialize in one or more subjects, and others serve as administrators. Some work full time in nonacademic settings and teach part time. Some lawyers become judges.

JUDGES

Judges apply the law and oversee the legal process in courts according to local, state, and federal statutes. They preside over cases concerning every aspect of society, from traffic offenses to disputes over management of professional sports, or from the rights of huge corporations to questions of disconnecting life-support equipment for terminally ill persons.

They must ensure that trials and hearings are conducted fairly, and that the court administers justice in a manner that safeguards the legal rights of all parties involved.

Judges preside over trials or hearings and listen as attorneys representing the parties present and argue their cases. They rule on the admissibility of evidence and methods of conducting testimony, and settle disputes between the opposing attorneys. They ensure that rules and procedures are followed, and if unusual circumstances arise for which standard procedures have not been established, judges direct how the trial will proceed based on their knowledge of the law.

Judges often hold pretrial hearings for cases. They listen to allegations and, based on the evidence presented, determine whether there is enough merit for a trial to be held. In criminal cases, judges may decide that persons charged with crimes should be held in jail pending their trial, or may set conditions for their release through the trial. In civil cases, judges may impose restrictions upon the parties until a trial is held.

When trials are held, juries are often selected to decide cases, including guilt or innocence in criminal cases, and the liability and the amount of compensation in civil cases. In these cases, judges instruct juries on applicable laws, direct them to deduce the facts from the evidence presented, and

hear their verdicts. However, judges decide cases when the law does not require a jury trial, or when the parties waive their right to a jury. In the absence of a jury, the judge determines guilt and imposes sentences in a criminal case; in civil cases, the judge rewards relief—such as compensation for damages—to the parties in the lawsuit (also called *litigants*).

Judges also work outside the courtroom *in chambers.* In their private offices, judges read documents on pleadings and motions, research legal issues, write opinions, and oversee the court's operations. Running a court is like running a small business, and judges also manage their court's administrative and clerical staff.

Judges' duties vary according to the extent of their jurisdictions and powers. *General trial court judges* of the federal and state court systems have jurisdiction over any case in their system. They generally try civil cases transcending the jurisdiction of lower courts, and all cases involving felony offenses. Federal and state *appellate court judges,* although few in number, have the power to overrule decisions made by trial court or administrative law judges if they determine that legal errors were made in a case, or if legal precedent does not support the judgment of the lower court. They rule on fewer cases and rarely have direct contact with litigants. Instead, they usually base their decisions on lower court records and written and oral arguments by lawyers.

Many state court judges preside in courts in which jurisdiction is limited by law to certain types of cases. A variety of titles are assigned to these judges, but among the most common are *municipal court judge, county court judge, magistrate,* and *justice of the peace.* Traffic violations, misdemeanors, small claims cases, and pretrial hearings constitute the bulk of the work of these judges, but some states allow them to handle cases involving domestic relations, probate, contracts, and other selected areas of the law.

Administrative law judges, formerly called *hearing officers,* are employed by government agencies to make determinations for administrative agencies. They make decisions on eligibility for various Social Security or worker's compensation benefits, enforcement of health and safety and environmental

protection regulations, employment discrimination cases, and compliance with economic regulatory requirements.

Working Conditions

Lawyers and judges do most of their work in offices, law libraries, and courtrooms. Lawyers sometimes meet in clients' homes or places of business and, when necessary, in hospitals or prisons. They may travel to attend meetings, gather evidence, and appear before courts, legislative bodies, and other authorities.

Salaried lawyers generally have structured work schedules. Lawyers in private practice may work irregular hours while conducting research, conferring with clients, or preparing briefs during nonoffice hours. Lawyers often work long hours, and about half regularly work 50 hours or more per week. They are under particularly heavy pressure, for example, when a case is being tried. Preparation for court includes keeping abreast of the latest laws and judicial decisions.

Although lawyers' work is not generally seasonal, the work of tax lawyers and other specialists may be an exception. Because lawyers in private practice can often determine their own workload and when they will retire, many stay in practice well beyond the usual retirement age.

Many judges work a standard 40-hour week, but a third of all judges work over 50 hours per week. Some judges with limited jurisdiction are employed part time and divide their time between their judicial responsibilities and other careers.

Employment

Lawyers held about 622,000 jobs in 1996; judges, about 78,000. About 7 out of 10 lawyers practiced privately, either in law firms or in solo practice. Most of the remaining lawyers held positions in government, the greatest number at the local

level. In the federal government, lawyers work for many different agencies but are concentrated in the Departments of Justice, Treasury, and Defense. Other lawyers are employed as house counsel by public utilities, banks, insurance companies, real estate agencies, manufacturing firms, welfare and religious organizations, and other business firms and nonprofit organizations. Some salaried lawyers also have part-time independent practices; others work as lawyers part time while working full time in another occupation.

All judges, magistrates, and other judicial workers were employed by federal, state, or local governments, with about 4 out of 10 holding positions in the federal government.

Law professors also hold law degrees, as do other professionals such as politicians, managers, and administrators.

*T*raining, Other Qualifications, and Advancement

LAWYERS

To practice law in the courts of any state or other jurisdiction, a person must be licensed, or admitted to its bar, under rules established by the jurisdiction's highest court. All require that applicants for admission to the bar pass a written bar examination; most jurisdictions also require that applicants pass a separate written ethics examination. Lawyers who have been admitted to the bar in one jurisdiction may occasionally be admitted to the bar in another without taking an examination if they meet that jurisdiction's standards of good moral character and have a specified period of legal experience. Federal courts and agencies set their own qualifications for those practicing before them.

To qualify for the bar examination in most states, an applicant must usually obtain a college degree and graduate from a law school accredited by the American Bar Association (ABA) or the proper state authorities. (ABA accreditation signifies that the law school—particularly its library and faculty—meets certain standards developed to promote quality legal education.) ABA currently accredits 179 law schools. Others are approved by state authorities only. With certain exceptions, graduates of schools not approved by the ABA are restricted to taking the bar examination and practicing in the state or other jurisdiction in which the school is located; most of these schools are in California. In 1997, seven states accepted the study of law in a law office or in combination with study in a law school; only California accepts the study of law by correspondence as qualifying applicants to take the bar examination. Several states require registration and approval of students by the State Board of Law Examiners, either before they enter law school or during their early years of legal study.

Although there is no nationwide bar examination, 47 states, the District of Columbia, Guam, the Northern Mariana Islands, and the Virgin Islands require the six-hour Multistate Bar Examination (MBE) as part of the bar examination; the MBE is not required in Indiana, Louisiana, Washington, and Puerto Rico. The MBE covers issues of broad interest, and is sometimes given in addition to a locally prepared state bar examination. The three-hour Multistate Essay Examination (MEE) is used as part of the state bar examination in a few states. States vary in their use of MBE and MEE scores.

Performance examinations to test practical skills of beginning lawyers are required by eight states. This program has been well received, and more states are expected to require performance testing in the future. Requirements vary by state, although the test usually is taken at the same time as the bar exam, and is a one-time requirement.

The required college and law school education usually takes seven years of full-time study after high school—four years of undergraduate study followed by three years in law school. Although some law schools accept a very small number of students after three years of college, most require applicants to have a bachelor's degree. To meet the needs of students who can attend only part time, a number of law schools have night or part-time divisions that usually require

four years of study; about one in ten graduates from ABA-approved schools attends part time.

Although there is no recommended prelaw major, prospective lawyers should develop proficiency in writing and speaking, reading, researching, analyzing, and thinking logically—skills needed to succeed both in law school and in the profession. Whatever the major, a multidisciplinary background is recommended. Courses in English, foreign language, public speaking, government, philosophy, history, economics, mathematics, and computer science, among others, are useful.

Students interested in a particular aspect of law may find related courses helpful. For example, prospective patent lawyers need a strong background in engineering or science, and future tax lawyers must have extensive knowledge of accounting.

Acceptance by most law schools depends on the applicant's ability to demonstrate an aptitude for the study of law, usually through good undergraduate grades, the Law School Admission Test (LSAT), the quality of the applicant's undergraduate school, any prior work experience, and sometimes a personal interview. However, law schools vary in the weight they place on each of these and other factors.

All law schools approved by the ABA, except for those in Puerto Rico, require applicants to take the LSAT. Nearly all law schools require applicants to have certified transcripts sent to the Law School Data Assembly Service, which then sends applicants' LSAT scores and their standardized records of college grades to the law schools of their choice. Both this service and the LSAT are administered by the Law School Admission Council.

Competition for admission to many law schools is intense. Enrollments in these schools rose very rapidly during the 1970s, with applicants far outnumbering available seats. The number of applicants decreased markedly in the 1990s, easing competition slightly; however, the number of applicants to most law schools still greatly exceeds the number that can be admitted. Competition for admission to the more prestigious law schools is always keen.

During the first year or year and a half of law school, students generally study fundamental courses such as constitutional law, contracts, property law, torts, civil procedure, and legal writing. In the remaining time, they may elect specialized courses in fields such as tax, labor, or corporation law. Law students often acquire practical experience by participation in school-sponsored legal clinic activities; in the school's moot court competitions, in which students conduct appellate arguments; in practice trials under the supervision of experienced lawyers and judges; and through research and writing on legal issues for the school's law journal.

In 1997, law students in 48 states were required to pass the Multistate Professional Responsibility Examination (MPRE), which tests their knowledge of the ABA codes on professional responsibility and judicial conduct. In some states, the MPRE may be taken during law school, usually after completing a course on legal ethics.

A number of law schools have clinical programs in which students gain legal experience through practice trials and law school projects under the supervision of practicing lawyers and law school faculty. Law school clinical programs might include work in legal aid clinics, for example, or on the staff of legislative committees. Part-time or summer clerkships in law firms, government agencies, and corporate legal departments also provide valuable experience. Such training can provide references or lead directly to a job after graduation, and can help students decide what kind of practice best suits them. Clerkships may also be an important source of financial aid.

Graduates receive the degree of *juris doctor* (J.D.) as the first professional degree. Advanced law degrees may be desirable for those planning to specialize, do research, or teach. Some law students pursue joint degree programs, which generally require an additional semester or year. Joint degree programs are offered in a number of areas, including law and business administration or public administration.

After graduation, lawyers must keep informed about legal and nonlegal developments that affect their practice. Currently, 37 states and jurisdictions mandate continuing legal

education (CLE). Many law schools and state and local bar associations provide continuing education courses that help lawyers stay abreast of recent developments. Some states allow CLE credits to be obtained through participation in seminars on the Internet.

The practice of law involves a great deal of responsibility. Individuals planning careers in law should like to work with people, and be able to win the respect and confidence of their clients, associates, and the public. Perseverance and reasoning ability are essential to analyze complex cases and reach sound conclusions. Lawyers also need creativity when handling new and unique legal problems.

Most beginning lawyers start in salaried positions. Newly hired salaried attorneys usually start as associates and work with more experienced lawyers or judges. After several years of progressively more responsible salaried employment, some lawyers are admitted to partnership in their firm, or go into practice for themselves. Some lawyers, after several years of practice, become full-time law school faculty members or administrators; a growing number have advanced degrees in other fields, as well.

Some attorneys use their legal training in administrative or managerial positions in various departments of large corporations. A transfer from a corporation's legal department to another department often is viewed as a way to gain administrative experience and rise in the ranks of management.

JUDGES

Most judges have first been lawyers. Federal and state judges are generally required to be lawyers. About 40 states allow nonlawyers to hold limited-jurisdiction judgeships, but opportunities are better with law experience. Federal administrative law judges must be lawyers and pass a competitive examination administered by the U.S. Office of Personnel Management. Some state administrative law judges and other hearing officials are not required to be lawyers, but law degrees are preferred for most positions.

Federal judges are appointed for life by the President, with the consent of the Senate. Federal administrative law judges are appointed by the various federal agencies and have virtually lifetime tenure. About half of all state judges are appointed, while the remainder are elected in partisan or non-partisan state elections. Many state and local judges serve fixed renewable terms, which range from 4 or 6 years for some trial court judgeships, to as long as 14 years or life for other trial or appellate court judges. Judicial nominating commissions, composed of members of the bar and the public, are used to screen candidates for judgeships in many states, as well as for some federal judgeships.

All states have some type of orientation for newly elected or appointed judges. The Federal Judicial Center, the ABA, the National Judicial College, and the National Center for State Courts provide judicial education and training for judges and other judicial branch personnel. General and continuing education courses usually run from a couple of days to three weeks in length. Over half of the states, including Puerto Rico, require judges to enroll in continuing education courses while serving on the bench.

*J*ob Outlook

Individuals interested in pursuing careers as lawyers or judges will encounter keen competition through the year 2006. The number of law school graduates is expected to continue to strain the economy's capacity to absorb them. As for judges, the prestige associated with serving on the bench should ensure continued, intense competition for openings.

LAWYERS

Employment of lawyers grew very rapidly from the early 1970s through the early 1990s, but has started to level off in the last several years. Employment is expected to grow about

as fast as the average for all occupations through the year 2006. Continuing demand for lawyers will result from growth in the population and the general level of business activities. Demand will also be spurred by growth of legal action in such areas as health care, intellectual property, international law, elder law, sexual harassment, and the environment. The wider availability and affordability of legal clinics and prepaid legal service programs should result in increased use of legal services by middle-income people.

Employment growth will be slower than in the past. In an effort to reduce the money spent on legal fees, many businesses are turning to large accounting firms to provide employee benefit counseling, process documents, and handle other services previously performed by law firms. Also, mediation and dispute resolution are increasingly being used as alternatives to litigation.

Competition for job openings will continue to be keen because of the large numbers graduating from law school each year. During the 1970s, the annual number of law school graduates more than doubled, outpacing the rapid growth of jobs. Growth in the yearly number of law school graduates slowed during the early to mid-1980s, but increased again in the late 1980s to early 1990s. Although graduates with superior academic records from well-regarded law schools will have more job opportunities, most graduates will encounter stiff competition for jobs. As in the past, some graduates may have to accept positions in areas outside their field of interest or for which they feel overqualified. They may choose to enter jobs for which legal training is an asset, but not normally a requirement—for example, administrative, managerial, and business positions in banks, insurance firms, real estate companies, government agencies, and other organizations.

Some recent law school graduates who are unable to find permanent positions are turning to the growing number of legal temporary staffing firms, which place attorneys in short-term jobs until they are able to secure full-time positions. This service allows companies to hire lawyers on an as-needed basis and allows beginning lawyers to develop practical skills while looking for permanent positions.

Due to the competition for jobs, a law graduate's geographic mobility and work experience assume greater importance. The willingness to relocate may be an advantage in getting a job, but to be licensed in a new state, a lawyer may have to take an additional state bar examination. In addition, employers increasingly seek graduates who have advanced law degrees and experience in a specialty such as tax, patent, or admiralty law.

Employment growth for lawyers will continue to be concentrated in salaried jobs, as businesses and all levels of government employ a growing number of staff attorneys, and as employment in the legal services industry grows in larger law firms. Most salaried positions are in urban areas where government agencies, law firms, and big corporations are concentrated. The number of self-employed lawyers is expected to increase slowly, reflecting the difficulty of establishing a profitable new practice in the face of competition from larger, established law firms. Also, the growing complexity of law, which encourages specialization, along with the cost of maintaining up-to-date legal research materials, favors larger firms.

For lawyers who wish to work independently, establishing a new practice will probably be easiest in small towns and expanding suburban areas, as long as an active market for legal services exists. In such communities, competition from larger established law firms is likely to be less than in big cities, and new lawyers may find it easier to become known to potential clients.

Some lawyers are adversely affected by cyclical swings in the economy. During recessions, the demand declines for some discretionary legal services, such as planning estates, drafting wills, and handling real estate transactions. Also, corporations are less likely to litigate cases when declining sales and profits result in budgetary restrictions. Some corporations and law firms will not hire new attorneys until business improves, or they may cut staff to contain costs. Several factors, however, mitigate the overall impact of recessions on lawyers. During recessions, individuals and corporations face other legal problems, such as bankruptcies, foreclosures, and divorces requiring legal action.

JUDGES

Employment of judges is expected to grow more slowly than the average for all occupations. Contradictory social forces affect the demand for judges. Growing public concerns about crime, safety, and efficient administration of justice should spur demand; on the other hand, tight public funding should slow job growth.

Competition for judgeships will remain keen. Most job openings will arise as judges retire. Traditionally, many judges have held their positions until late in life. Now, early retirement is becoming more common, creating more job openings. However, becoming a judge will still be difficult. Besides competing with other qualified people, judicial candidates must gain political support in order to be elected or appointed.

*E*arnings

Median salaries of lawyers six months after graduation from law school in 1996 varied by type of work, as indicated by Table 4-1.

TABLE 4-1
Median Salaries of Lawyers Six Months
after Graduation, 1996

All graduates	$40,000
Private practice	50,000
Business/industry	45,000
Academe	35,000
Judicial clerkship	35,000
Government	34,500
Public interest	30,000

Source: National Association for Law Placement.

Salaries of experienced attorneys also vary widely according to the type, size, and location of their employer. The median annual salary of all lawyers was about $60,000 in 1996. General attorneys in the federal government averaged around $72,700 a year in 1997; the relatively small number of patent attorneys in the federal government averaged around $81,600.

Lawyers who practice alone usually earn less than those who are partners in law firms. Lawyers starting their own practice may need to work part time in other occupations to supplement their income until their practice is well established.

According to the Administrative Office of the U.S. Courts, federal district court judges had salaries of $133,600 in 1997, as did judges in the Court of Federal Claims; circuit court judges earned $141,700 a year. Federal judges with limited jurisdiction, such as magistrates and bankruptcy court judges, had salaries of $122,900. Full-time federal administrative law judges had average salaries of $94,800. The Chief Justice of the U.S. Supreme Court earned $171,500, and the Associate Justices earned $164,100.

According to a survey by the National Center for State Courts, annual salaries of associate justices of states' highest courts averaged $101,800 in 1997, and ranged from about $68,900 to $133,600. Salaries of state intermediate appellate court judges averaged $91,000, and ranged from $79,400 to $124,200. Salaries of state judges with limited jurisdiction vary widely; some salaries are set locally.

Most salaried lawyers and judges are provided health and life insurance, and contributions are made on their behalf to retirement plans. Lawyers who practice independently are covered only if they arrange and pay for such benefits themselves.

Related Occupations

Legal training is useful in many other occupations. Some of these are arbitrator, mediator, journalist, patent agent, title

examiner, legislative assistant, lobbyist, FBI special agent, political office holder, and corporate executive.

Sources of Additional Information

Information on law schools and law as a career may be obtained from:

American Bar Association
750 North Lake Shore Drive
Chicago, IL 60611

Information on the LSAT, the Law School Data Assembly Service, applying to law school, and financial aid for law students may be obtained from:

Law School Admission Council
P.O. Box 40
Newtown, PA 18940
Homepage: www.lsac.org

Information on acquiring a job as a lawyer with the federal government may be obtained from the Office of Personnel Management through a telephone-based system. Consult your telephone directory under "U.S. Government" for a local number or call (912) 757-3000 [TDD (912) 744-2299]. That number is not toll-free and charges may result. Information also is available from the OPM's Internet site: www.usajobs.opm.gov.

The specific requirements for admission to the bar in a particular state or other jurisdiction may also be obtained at the state capital from the clerk of the state Supreme Court or the administrator of the state Board of Bar Examiners.

CHAPTER 5

Working as a Correctional Officer

Significant Points

- Correctional officers held about 320,000 jobs in 1996. About 11,000 correctional officers worked at federal correctional institutions, and about 5,100 worked in privately owned and managed prisons.

- A 1996 survey found the average correctional officer earning $26,100, although some states and the federal government pay considerably more than that.

- Most correctional officer positions require only a high school diploma, although a two- or four-year college degree is being increasingly required in a growing number of jurisdictions.

- Job opportunities in corrections are expected to be plentiful due to much faster than average employment growth coupled with high turnover.

The material in this chapter is adapted from Bureau of Labor Statistics, 1998–1999 *Occupational Outlook Handbook*.

*N*ature of the Work

Correctional officers are responsible for overseeing individuals who have been arrested, are awaiting trial or other hearings, or who have been convicted of a crime and sentenced to serve time in a jail, reformatory, or penitentiary. They maintain security and observe inmate conduct and behavior to prevent disturbances and escapes.

Correctional officers' duties differ with the setting in which they are performed. The majority of the approximately 3,300 jails in the United States are operated by county governments, with about three-quarters of all jails under the jurisdiction of an elected sheriff. Duty in jails differs from that in prisons in a number of important ways. For instance, the jail population changes constantly. The American jail system processes more than 22 million people a year, with about half a million inmates in jail at any given time. Approximately 1 million inmates are incarcerated in federal and state prisons. The prison population, by contrast, is far more stable.

Many correctional officers are employed by police and sheriffs departments in county and municipal jails or precinct station houses. These officers often have no law enforcement responsibilities outside the jail. (See Chapter 9, "Working as a Law Enforcement Officer," in this guide.) Others are employed by large regional jails or state and federal prisons where job duties are specialized. A relatively small number supervise aliens being held by the Immigration and Naturalization Service before being released or deported. Regardless of the setting, correctional officers maintain order within the institution, enforce rules and regulations, and may supplement whatever counseling inmates receive.

To make sure inmates are orderly and obey rules, correctional officers monitor inmates' activities, including working, exercising, eating, and showering. They assign and supervise inmates' work assignments. Sometimes it is necessary for them to search inmates and their living quarters for weapons or drugs, to settle disputes between inmates, and to enforce

discipline. Correctional officers cannot show favoritism and must report any inmate who violates the rules. A few officers in prison settings hold security positions in towers, where they are equipped with high-powered rifles. In both jail and prison facilities with direct-supervision cell blocks, officers are unarmed—they are locked in a cell block alone, or with another officer, among the 50 to 100 inmates who reside there. The officers enforce regulations primarily through their interpersonal communications skills, although they may have inmates who do not obey their orders transferred to facilities with less desirable living arrangements and fewer privileges.

Correctional officers periodically inspect the facilities. They may, for example, check cells and other areas of the institution for unsanitary conditions, weapons, drugs, fire hazards, and any evidence of infractions of the rules. In addition, they routinely inspect locks, window bars, grille doors, and gates for signs of tampering.

Correctional officers report orally and in writing on inmate conduct and on the quality and quantity of work done by inmates. Officers also report disturbances, violations of rules, and any unusual occurrences. They usually keep a daily record of their activities. In the most high-security facilities where the most dangerous inmates are housed, correctional officers can monitor the activities of prisoners from a centralized control center with the aid of closed-circuit television cameras and a computer tracking system. In such an environment, the inmates may not see anyone but officers for days or weeks at a time and may only rarely leave their cells.

Depending on the offender's security classification within the institution, correctional officers may have to escort inmates to and from cells and other areas and accompany them to see authorized visitors. Officers may also escort prisoners between the institution and courtrooms, medical facilities, and other destinations. Officers inspect mail and visitors for prohibited items. Should the situation arise, they assist the responsible law enforcement authorities by helping to

investigate crimes committed within the institution or by helping to search for escaped inmates.

Correctional sergeants directly supervise correctional officers. They usually are responsible for maintaining security and for directing the activities of a group of inmates during an assigned shift or in an assigned area.

Working Conditions

Correctional officers may work indoors or outdoors, depending on their specific duties. Some correctional institutions are well lighted, temperature controlled, and ventilated, but many others are overcrowded, hot, and noisy. Outdoors, weather conditions may be disagreeable—for example, when standing watch on a guard tower in cold weather. Working in a correctional institution can be stressful and hazardous; correctional officers occasionally are injured in confrontations with inmates who may feel that they have little to lose from violent behavior.

Correctional officers usually work an eight-hour day, five days a week, on rotating shifts. Prison security must be provided around the clock, which often means that junior officers work weekends, holidays, and nights. In addition, officers may be required to work paid overtime.

Employment

Correctional officers held about 320,000 jobs in 1996. Six of every ten worked in state correctional institutions such as prisons, prison camps, and reformatories. Most of the remainder worked in city and county jails or other institutions run by local governments. About 11,000 correctional officers worked in federal correctional institutions, and about 5,100 worked in privately owned and managed prisons.

Most correctional officers work in relatively large institutions located in rural areas, although a significant number work in jails and other smaller facilities located in law enforcement agencies throughout the country.

*T*raining, Other Qualifications, and Advancement

Most institutions require that correctional officers be at least 18 or 21 years of age, have a high school education or its equivalent, have no felony convictions, and be a U.S. citizen. In addition, correctional institutions increasingly seek correctional officers with postsecondary education, particularly in psychology, criminal justice, police science, criminology, and related fields.

Correctional officers must be in good health. The federal system and many states require candidates to meet formal standards of physical fitness, eyesight, and hearing. Strength, good judgment, and the ability to think and act quickly are indispensable. The federal system and some states screen applicants for drug abuse and require candidates to pass a written or oral examination, along with a background check.

Federal, state, and some local departments of corrections provide training for correctional officers based on guidelines established by the American Correctional Association, the American Jail Association, and other professional organizations. Some states have regional training academies, which are available to local agencies. All states and local departments of correction provide on-the-job training at the conclusion of formal instruction. Officer trainees receive several weeks or months of training in an actual job setting under the supervision of an experienced officer. Entry requirements and on-the-job training vary widely from agency to agency.

Academy trainees generally receive instruction on institutional policies, regulations, and operations, as well as on cus-

tody and security procedures, among other subjects. New federal correctional officers must undergo 200 hours of formal training within the first year of employment. They must complete 120 hours of specialized correctional instruction at the federal Bureau of Prisons residential training center at Glynco, Georgia, within the first 60 days after appointment. Experienced officers receive in-service training to keep abreast of new ideas and procedures.

Correctional officers have the opportunity to join prison tactical response teams, which are trained to respond to riots, hostage situations, forced cell moves, and other potentially dangerous confrontations. Team members often receive monthly training and practice with weapons, chemical agents, forced-entry methods, and other tactics.

With education, experience, and training, qualified officers may advance to correctional sergeant or other supervisory or administrative positions. Many correctional institutions require experience as a correctional officer for other corrections positions. Ambitious correctional officers can be promoted all the way up to warden. Officers sometimes transfer to related areas, such as parole officer positions.

$\mathcal{J}$ob Outlook

Job opportunities for correctional officers are expected to be favorable through the year 2006. The need to replace correctional officers who transfer to other occupations or leave the labor force, coupled with rising employment demand, will generate many thousands of job openings each year. In addition, some local and a few state correctional agencies have traditionally experienced difficulty in attracting qualified applicants, largely due to relatively low salaries and the concentration of jobs in rural locations. This situation is expected to continue.

Employment of correctional officers is expected to increase faster than the average for all occupations through the year 2006 as additional officers are hired to supervise and control

a growing inmate population. Increasing public concern about the spread of crime and illegal drugs—resulting in more police making more arrests and getting more convictions—and the adoption of mandatory sentencing guidelines calling for longer sentences and reduced parole for inmates will spur demand for correctional officers. Expansion and new construction of correctional facilities also are expected to create many new jobs for correctional officers, although state and local government budgetary constraints could affect the rate at which new facilities are built and staffed. Some employment opportunities also may arise in the private sector as public authorities opt to contract with private companies to provide and staff corrections facilities.

Layoffs of correctional officers are rare because security must be maintained in correctional institutions at all times.

*E*arnings

According to a 1996 survey in *Corrections Compendium,* a national journal for corrections professionals, federal and state correctional officers' annual salaries averaged about $26,100 and ranged from a low of $17,300 in South Carolina to a high of $41,700 in Rhode Island.

At the federal level, the starting salary was about $20,200 to $22,600 a year in 1996; supervisory correctional officers started at about $28,300 a year. Starting salaries were slightly higher in selected areas where prevailing local pay levels were higher. The annual average salary for correctional officers employed by the federal government was $33,540 in early 1997.

Correctional officers employed in the public sector usually are provided uniforms or a clothing allowance to purchase their own uniforms. Most are provided or can participate in hospitalization or major medical insurance plans; many officers can get disability and life insurance at group rates. They also receive vacation and sick leave and pension benefits. Officers employed by the federal government and most state gov-

ernments are covered by civil service systems or merit boards. Their retirement coverage entitles them to retire at age 50 after 20 years of service or at any age with 25 years of service. In the federal system and some states, many correctional officers are represented by labor unions.

Related Occupations

A number of related careers are open to high school graduates who are interested in protective services and the field of security. Bodyguards escort people and protect them from injury or invasion of privacy. House or store detectives patrol business establishments to protect against theft and vandalism and to enforce standards of good behavior. Security guards protect government, commercial, and industrial property against theft, vandalism, illegal entry, and fire. Police officers and deputy sheriffs maintain law and order, prevent crime, and arrest offenders. Probation and parole officers monitor and counsel offenders and evaluate their progress in becoming productive members of society.

Sources of Additional Information

Information about entrance requirements, training, and career opportunities for correctional officers on the state and local levels may be obtained from state departments of corrections or nearby correctional institutions and facilities, including police departments and county sheriff offices.
Other sources of information include:

American Correctional Association
4380 Forbes Boulevard
Lanham, MD 20706-4322
Phone: (800) 222-5646

American Jail Association
2053 Day Road, Suite 100
Hagerstown, MD 21740
Phone: (301) 790-3930

Information on entrance requirements, training, and career opportunities for correctional officers on the federal level may be obtained by calling the federal Bureau of Prisons. Regional recruitment offices have toll-free telephone numbers listed in local phone directories. In addition, information on obtaining a job with the federal government may be obtained from the Office of Personnel Management through a telephone-based system. Consult your telephone directory under "U.S. Government" for a local number or call (912) 757-3000 [TDD (912) 744-2299]. The number is not toll-free and charges may result. Information also is available from the OPM's Internet site: www.usajobs.opm.gov.

CHAPTER 6

Working as a Firefighter

Significant Points

- Firefighters held about 293,000 jobs in 1996. More than nine of every ten worked in municipal or county fire departments.

- Firefighting attracts many people because a high school education is usually sufficient, and earnings are above average. In recent years, however, an increasing proportion of entrants to this occupation have some postsecondary education.

- Median weekly earnings for firefighting occupations were around $658 in 1996, while the highest 10 percent earned more than $979. The average annual salary for all firefighters in the federal government in nonsupervisory, supervisory, and managerial positions was about $28,800

The material in this chapter is adapted from Bureau of Labor Statistics, 1998–1999 *Occupational Outlook Handbook*.

in 1996. Fire lieutenants and fire captains may earn considerably more.

- Keen competition for firefighting positions is expected.

*N*ature of the Work

Firefighters respond to a variety of emergency situations in which life, property, or the environment are at risk. They are frequently the first emergency response team at the scene of an accident, fire, flood, earthquake, or act of terrorism. Every year, fires and other emergency conditions take thousands of lives and destroy property worth billions of dollars. Firefighters help protect the public against these dangers. This statement provides information only about career firefighters; it does not cover volunteer firefighters, who perform the same duties, and who may comprise the majority of firefighters in a residential area.

Most calls to which firefighters respond involve medical emergencies, and many fire departments provide ambulance service for victims. Firefighters receive training in emergency medical procedures, and many fire departments require them to be certified as emergency medical technicians.

During duty hours, firefighters must be prepared to respond immediately to a fire or any other emergency situation that arises. Each situation a firefighter encounters is unique. Because firefighting is dangerous and complex, it requires organization and teamwork. At every emergency scene, firefighters perform specific duties assigned by a superior officer. They may connect hose lines to hydrants, operate a pump or other equipment, or position ladders. They may rescue victims and administer emergency medical aid, ventilate smoke-filled areas, and salvage the contents of buildings. Their duties may change several times while the company is in action. Sometimes they remain at the site of a disaster for several days or more, rescuing survivors and assisting with medical emergencies.

The job of firefighter has become more complicated in recent years due to the use of increasingly sophisticated equipment and the need to assume a wider range of responsibilities. These responsibilities include emergency medical treatment, assisting in the recovery from natural disasters such as earthquakes and tornadoes, and the control, prevention, and cleanup of oil spills and other hazardous-materials incidents.

Firefighters are primarily involved with protecting business and residential structures, but they also work at airports on crash and rescue crews, at chemical plants, by waterfronts, and in forests and wilderness areas. In forests, air patrols locate fires and report their findings to headquarters by telephone or radio. Fire rangers patrol areas of the forest to locate and report fires and hazardous conditions and to ensure that travelers and campers comply with fire regulations. When fires break out, firefighters use hand tools and water hoses to battle the blaze. Some specialized firefighters parachute from airplanes when necessary to reach inaccessible areas.

Most fire departments have a fire-prevention division, usually headed by a fire marshal. Fire inspectors conduct inspections of structures to prevent fires and ensure fire-code compliance. These firefighters may also work with developers and planners to check and approve plans for new buildings. Fire prevention personnel often speak on these subjects before public assemblies and civic organizations. Some firefighters become fire investigators, who determine the origin and causes of fires. They collect evidence, interview witnesses, and prepare reports on fires in cases where the cause may be arson or criminal negligence. Some investigators have police powers and may arrest suspects. They may also be called upon to testify in court.

Between alarms, firefighters participate in educational activities. In addition to taking classes themselves, they sometimes give lectures or demonstrations on safety issues to the local community. They may also clean and maintain equipment, conduct practice drills and fire inspections, and participate in physical fitness activities. They prepare written

reports on fire incidents and review fire-science literature to keep abreast of technological developments and changing administrative practices and policies.

Working Conditions

Firefighters spend much of their time at fire stations, which usually have features common to a residential facility. When an alarm comes in, firefighters must respond rapidly, regardless of the weather or the hour. They may spend long periods on their feet, sometimes in adverse weather, tending to fires, medical emergencies, hazardous-materials incidents, and other emergencies.

Firefighting is a very hazardous occupation. It involves risk of death or injury from sudden cave-ins of floors or toppling walls, and from exposure to flames and smoke. Strong winds and falling trees and branches can make fighting forest fires particularly dangerous. Firefighters may also come in contact with poisonous, flammable, or explosive gases and chemicals, or radioactive or other hazardous materials that may have immediate or long-term effects on their health. For these reasons, they must wear appropriate protective gear, which can be very heavy.

Work hours of firefighters are longer and vary more widely than hours of most other workers. Many work more than 50 hours a week. During some weeks, they may work significantly longer hours. In some cities, they are on duty for 24 hours, then off for 48 hours, and receive an extra day off at intervals. In other cities, they work a day shift of 10 hours for 3 or 4 days, a night shift of 14 hours for 3 or 4 nights, have 3 or 4 days off, and then repeat the cycle. In addition, firefighters often work extra hours at fires and other emergencies and are regularly assigned to work on holidays. Fire lieutenants and fire captains often work the same hours as the firefighters they supervise. Duty hours include time when firefighters study, train, and perform fire-prevention duties.

*E*mployment

Firefighters held about 293,000 jobs in 1996. More than nine of every ten worked in municipal or county fire departments. Some very large cities have several thousand firefighters, while many small towns have only a few. Most of the remainder worked in fire departments on federal and state installations, including airports. Private firefighting companies employ a small number of firefighters.

*T*raining, Other Qualifications, and Advancement

Applicants for municipal firefighting jobs may have to pass a written test; tests of strength, physical stamina, coordination, and agility; and a medical examination, including a drug screening. Workers also may be monitored on a random basis for drug use after accepting employment. Examinations are generally open to persons who are at least 18 years of age and have a high school education or the equivalent. Those who receive the highest scores in all phases of testing have the best chances for appointment. The completion of community college courses in fire science may improve an applicant's chances for appointment. In recent years, an increasing proportion of entrants to this occupation have some postsecondary education.

As a rule, beginners in large fire departments are trained for several weeks at the department's training center. Through classroom instruction and practical training, the recruits study firefighting techniques, fire prevention, hazardous materials, local building codes, and emergency medical procedures, including first aid and cardiopulmonary resuscitation. They also learn how to use axes, saws, fire extinguishers, ladders, and other firefighting and rescue equipment. After successfully completing this training, they

are assigned to a fire company, where they undergo a period of probation.

A number of fire departments have accredited apprenticeship programs lasting up to five years. These programs combine formal, technical instruction with on-the-job training under the supervision of experienced firefighters. Technical instruction covers subjects such as firefighting techniques and equipment, chemical hazards associated with various combustible building materials, emergency medical procedures, and fire prevention and safety.

Most experienced firefighters continue studying to improve their job performance and prepare for promotion examinations. Today, firefighters need more training to operate increasingly sophisticated equipment, and to deal safely with the greater hazards associated with fighting fires in larger, more complex structures. To progress to higher-level positions, they must acquire expertise in the most advanced firefighting equipment and techniques and in building construction, emergency medical technology, writing, public speaking, management and budgeting procedures, and labor relations. Fire departments frequently conduct training programs, and some firefighters attend training sessions sponsored by the National Fire Academy. These training sessions cover various topics, including executive development, antiarson techniques, disaster preparedness, hazardous-materials control, and public fire safety and education. Some states also have extensive firefighter training and certification programs.

Many colleges and universities offer courses leading to two- or four-year degrees in fire engineering or fire science. Many fire departments offer firefighters incentives such as tuition reimbursement or higher pay for completing advanced training.

Among the personal qualities firefighters need are mental alertness, self-discipline, courage, mechanical aptitude, endurance, strength, and a sense of public service. Initiative and good judgment are extremely important because firefighters independently make quick decisions in emergencies. Because members of a crew live and work closely together under conditions of stress and danger for extended periods, they should be dependable and able to get along well with others in a group. Leadership qualities are necessary for officers, who must establish and maintain discipline and efficiency, as well as direct the activities of firefighters in their companies.

Opportunities for promotion are good in most fire departments. As firefighters gain expertise, they may advance to a higher rank. The line of promotion is usually to engineer, lieutenant, captain, battalion chief, assistant chief, deputy chief, and finally to chief. Advancement generally depends upon scores on a written examination, job performance, interviews, and seniority. Increasingly, fire departments are using assessment centers, which simulate a variety of actual job performance tasks, to screen for the best candidates for promotion. Many fire departments now require a bachelor's degree, preferably in fire science, public administration, or a related field, for promotion to positions higher than battalion chief. Some departments also require a master's degree for the chief, as well as for executive fire officer certification from the National Fire Academy, and for state chief officer certification.

Job Outlook

Firefighters are expected to face keen competition for available job openings. Firefighting attracts many people because a high school education is usually sufficient, earnings are relatively high, and a pension is guaranteed upon retirement. In addition, the work is frequently exciting and challenging and affords an opportunity to perform a valuable public service. Consequently, the number of qualified applicants in most areas generally exceeds the number of job openings, even though the written examination and physical requirements eliminate many applicants. This situation is expected to persist through the year 2006.

Employment of firefighters is expected to increase more slowly than the average for all occupations through the year 2006, as fire departments continue to compete with other public service providers for funding. Most growth in employ-

ment will be due to an expected increase in the number of paid firefighter positions versus volunteer firefighters, because the increased level of specialized training required in this occupation makes it more difficult for volunteer firefighters to remain qualified. Little employment growth is expected in large, urban fire departments. A small number of local governments are expected to contract with private companies for firefighting services.

In response to the expanding role of firefighters, some municipalities have combined fire prevention, public fire education, safety, and emergency medical services into a single organization commonly referred to as a *public safety organization*. Some local and regional fire departments are being consolidated into countywide establishments in order to cut overhead, take advantage of economies of scale, reduce administrative staffs, and establish consistent training standards and work procedures.

Turnover of firefighter jobs is unusually low, particularly for a hazardous occupation that requires a relatively limited investment in formal education. Nevertheless, most job openings are expected to result from the need to replace those who retire, stop working for other reasons, or transfer to other occupations.

Layoffs of firefighters are not common. Fire protection is an essential service, and citizens are likely to exert considerable pressure on city officials to expand or at least preserve the level of fire-protection coverage. Even when budget cuts do occur, local fire departments usually cut expenses by postponing equipment purchases or not hiring new firefighters, rather than by laying off staff.

$\mathcal{E}$arnings

Median weekly earnings for firefighting occupations were around $658 in 1996. The middle 50 percent earned between $513 and $832 weekly. The lowest 10 percent earned less than $387, while the highest 10 percent earned more than $979.

The average annual salary for all firefighters in the federal government in nonsupervisory, supervisory, and managerial positions was about $28,800 in 1996. Fire lieutenants and fire captains may earn considerably more.

Firefighters who average 53 or more hours a week during their work period, which ranges from 7 to 28 days, are required to be paid overtime. Firefighters often earn overtime for working extra shifts to maintain minimum staffing levels, or for special emergencies.

Firefighters usually receive benefits including medical and liability insurance, vacation and sick leave, and some paid holidays. Almost all fire departments provide protective clothing (helmets, boots, and coats) and breathing apparatus, and many also provide dress uniforms. Firefighters are generally covered by pension plans, often providing retirement at half pay after 25 years of service or if disabled in the line of duty.

Many career firefighters and company officers are unionized, and belong to the International Association of Firefighters. Many chief officers belong to the International Association of Fire Chiefs.

*R*elated Occupations

An occupation closely related to fire protection is fire-protection engineer, in which the engineer identifies fire hazards in homes and workplaces, and designs prevention programs and automatic fire detection and extinguishing systems. Other occupations in which workers respond to emergencies include police officers and emergency medical technicians.

*S*ources of Additional Information

Information about a career as a firefighter may be obtained from local fire departments and:

International Association of Firefighters
1750 New York Ave. NW
Washington, DC 20006

U.S. Fire Administration
16825 South Seton Ave.
Emmitsburg, MD 21727

Information about firefighter professional qualifications
and a list of colleges and universities offering two- or four-
year degree programs in fire science or fire prevention may be
obtained from:

National Fire Protection Association
1 Batterymarch Park
Quincy, MA 02269

National Fire Academy
Degrees at a Distance Program
16825 South Seton Ave.
Emmitsburg, MD 21727

CHAPTER 7

Working as an Inspector or Compliance Officer

*S*ignificant Points

- Over 80 percent of the jobs discussed in this chapter are in federal, state, and local government agencies that inspect and enforce rules on matters such as health, safety, food, licensing, or finance.
- Inspectors and compliance officers held about 163,000 jobs throughout the United States in 1996.
- Because responsibilities vary, ranging from those of aviation safety inspectors to food inspectors, for example, training requirements, salary, and working conditions vary greatly.

The material in this chapter is adapted from Bureau of Labor Statistics, 1998–1999 *Occupational Outlook Handbook*.

*N*ature of the Work

Inspectors and compliance officers enforce a wide range of laws, regulations, policies, or procedures. They inspect and enforce rules on matters such as health, safety, food, licensing, or finance. Inspectors' and compliance officers' duties vary widely.

Agricultural commodity graders apply quality standards to aid the buying and selling of commodities, and to ensure that retailers and consumers know the quality of the products they purchase. Although this grading is not required by law, buyers may not be willing to purchase ungraded commodities. Graders usually specialize in an area such as eggs, meat, poultry, processed or fresh fruits and vegetables, grain, tobacco, cotton, or dairy products. They examine product samples to determine quality and grade, and issue official grading certificates. To maintain sanitation standards, graders may inspect the plant and equipment used in processing.

Attendance officers investigate continued absences of pupils from public schools.

Aviation safety inspectors ensure that Federal Aviation Administration (FAA) regulations that govern the quality, performance, and safety of aircraft equipment, aircraft operations, and personnel are adhered to. Aviation safety inspectors may inspect aircraft and equipment manufacturing, maintenance and repair, or flight procedures. They may work in the areas of flight operations, maintenance, or avionics, and usually specialize in either commercial or general aviation aircraft. They also examine and certify aircraft pilots, pilot examiners, flight instructors, repair stations, schools, and instructional materials.

Bank examiners investigate financial institutions to enforce federal or state laws and regulations governing the institution's operations and solvency. Examiners schedule audits, determine actions protecting the institution's solvency and the interests of shareholders and depositors, and recommend acceptance or rejection of applications for mergers, acquisitions, or establishment of a new institution.

Consumer safety inspectors and *officers* inspect food, feeds, pesticides, weights and measures, biological products, cosmetics, drugs, medical equipment, and radiation-emitting products. Some are proficient in several areas. Working individually or in teams under a senior inspector, they check on firms that produce, handle, store, or market the products they regulate. They ensure that standards are maintained and respond to consumer complaints by questioning employees, vendors, and others to obtain evidence. Inspectors look for inaccurate product labeling, and for decomposition or chemical or bacteriological contamination that could result in a product becoming harmful to health. They may use portable scales, cameras, ultraviolet lights, thermometers, chemical testing kits, radiation monitors, or other equipment to find violations. They may send product samples, collected as part of their examinations, to laboratories for analysis.

After completing their inspections, inspectors discuss their observations with plant managers or officials, and point out areas where corrective measures are needed. They write reports of their findings and, when necessary, compile evidence for use in court if legal action must be taken.

Customs inspectors enforce laws governing imports and exports. Stationed in the United States and overseas at airports, seaports, and border crossing points, they examine, count, weigh, gauge, measure, and sample commercial and noncommercial cargoes entering and leaving the United States, to determine admissibility and the amount of duties that must be paid. They ensure that all cargo is properly described on accompanying importers' declarations to determine the proper duty and to interdict contraband. They inspect baggage and articles carried by passengers and crew members to ensure that all merchandise is declared, proper duties are paid, and contraband is not present. They also ensure that people, ships, planes, and anything used to import or export cargo comply with all appropriate entrance and clearance requirements.

Dealer compliance representatives inspect franchised establishments, such as motels and fast-food restaurants, to ensure compliance with the franchiser's policies and procedures.

They may suggest changes in financial or other operations which, if not followed, can result in loss of the franchise.

Environmental health inspectors, who work primarily for state and local governments, ensure that food, water, and air meet government standards. They check the cleanliness and safety of food and beverages produced in dairies and processing plants, or served in restaurants, hospitals, and other institutions. They often examine the handling, processing, and serving of food for compliance with sanitation rules and regulations, and oversee the treatment and disposal of sewage, refuse, and garbage. In addition, inspectors may visit pollution sources and test for pollutants by collecting air, water, or waste samples for analysis. They try to determine the nature and cause of pollution and initiate action to stop it.

In large local and state health or agriculture departments, environmental health inspectors may specialize in the areas of milk and dairy products, food sanitation, waste control, air pollution, water pollution, institutional sanitation, or occupational health. In rural areas and small towns, they may be responsible for a wide range of environmental health activities.

Equal opportunity representatives ascertain and correct unfair employment practices through consultation with and mediation between employers and minority groups.

Federal and state laws require *food inspectors* to inspect meat, poultry, their by-products, and egg products to ensure that they are safe for public consumption. Working onsite, frequently as part of a team, they inspect meat and poultry slaughtering, processing, and packaging operations, as well as egg-products operations. They also check for correct product labeling and proper sanitation.

Immigration inspectors interview and examine people seeking entrance to the United States and its territories. They inspect passports to determine whether people are legally eligible to enter and verify their citizenship status and identity. Immigration inspectors also prepare reports, maintain records, and process applications and petitions for immigration or temporary residence in the United States.

Logging operations inspectors review contract logging operations. They prepare reports and issue remedial instructions

for violations of contractual agreements and of fire and safety regulations.

Mine safety and health inspectors work to ensure the health and safety of miners. They visit mines and related facilities to obtain information on health and safety conditions and to enforce safety laws and regulations. They discuss their findings with the management of the mines and issue citations describing violations and hazards that must be corrected. Mine inspectors also investigate and report on mine accidents and may direct rescue and firefighting operations when fires or explosions occur.

Motor vehicle inspectors verify the compliance of automobiles and trucks with state requirements for safe operation and emissions. They inspect truck cargoes to assure compliance with legal limitations on gross weight and hazardous cargoes.

Occupational safety and health inspectors visit places of employment to detect unsafe machinery and equipment or unhealthy working conditions. They discuss their findings with the employers or plant managers and order that violations be promptly corrected in accordance with federal, state, or local government safety standards and regulations. They interview supervisors and employees in response to complaints or accidents, and may order suspension of activities posing threats to workers.

Park rangers enforce laws and regulations in state and national parks. Their duties range from registering vehicles and visitors, collecting fees, and providing information regarding park use and points of interest, to patrolling areas to prevent fires, participating in first-aid and rescue activities, and training and supervising other park workers. Some rangers specialize in snow safety and avalanche control. With increasing numbers of visitors to our national parks, some rangers specialize as law enforcement officers.

Postal inspectors observe the functioning of the postal system and enforce laws and regulations. As law enforcement agents, postal inspectors have statutory powers of arrest and the authority to carry firearms. They investigate criminal activities such as theft and misuse of the mail. In instances of

suspected mismanagement or fraud, inspectors conduct management or financial audits. They also collaborate with other government agencies, such as the Internal Revenue Service, as members of special task forces.

Railroad inspectors verify the compliance of railroad systems and equipment with federal safety regulations. They investigate accidents and review railroads' operating practices.

Revenue officers investigate and collect delinquent tax returns from individuals or businesses. They investigate leads from various sources. They attempt to resolve tax problems with taxpayers, recommend penalties and collection actions, and recommend criminal prosecutions when necessary.

Securities compliance examiners implement regulations concerning securities and real estate transactions. They investigate applications for registration of securities sales and complaints of irregular securities transactions, and recommend legal action when necessary.

Travel accommodations raters inspect hotels, motels, restaurants, campgrounds, and vacation resorts. They evaluate travel and tourist accommodations for travel guide publishers and organizations such as tourism promoters and automobile clubs.

Other inspectors and compliance officers include coroners, code inspectors, mortician investigators, and dealer-compliance representatives. Closely related work is done by construction and building inspectors.

Working Conditions

Inspectors and compliance officers meet all kinds of people and work in a variety of environments. Their jobs often involve considerable field work, and some inspectors travel frequently. They are generally furnished with an automobile or are reimbursed for travel expenses.

Inspectors may experience unpleasant, stressful, and dangerous working conditions. For example, mine safety and

health inspectors are exposed to the same hazards as miners. Some food inspectors examine and inspect the livestock-slaughtering process in slaughterhouses and frequently come in contact with unpleasant conditions. Postal inspectors have to put up with the stress inherent in all law enforcement work, in addition to the danger inherent in making occasional arrests. Park rangers often work outdoors—in many cases, on rugged terrain—in very hot or bitterly cold weather for extended periods.

Many inspectors work long and often irregular hours. Even those inspectors not engaged in some form of law enforcement may find themselves in adversarial roles when the organization or individual being inspected objects to the inspection.

*E*mployment

Inspectors and compliance officers held about 163,000 jobs in 1996. State governments employed 34 percent, the federal government—chiefly the Departments of Defense, Labor, Treasury, and Agriculture—employed 31 percent, and local governments employed 18 percent. The remaining 17 percent were employed throughout the private sector—primarily in education, hospitals, insurance companies, labor unions, and manufacturing firms.

Some consumer safety inspectors work for the U.S. Food and Drug Administration, but the majority of these inspectors work for state governments. Most food inspectors and agricultural commodity graders are employed by the U.S. Department of Agriculture. Many health inspectors work for state and local governments. Compliance inspectors are employed primarily by the Treasury and Labor departments on the federal level, as well as by state and local governments. The Department of Defense employs the most quality-assurance inspectors. The states and the Treasury Department employ internal revenue officers. Aviation safety inspectors work for the Federal Aviation Administration. The Environmental Pro-

tection Agency employs inspectors to verify compliance with pollution control and other laws. The U.S. Department of Labor and many state governments employ occupational safety and health inspectors, equal opportunity officers, and mine safety and health inspectors. The U.S. Department of Interior employs park rangers. Department of the Treasury customs inspectors work in the United States and overseas at airports, seaports, and border crossing points.

Training, Other Qualifications, and Advancement

Because of the diversity of the functions they perform, qualifications for inspector and compliance officer jobs differ greatly. Requirements include a combination of education, experience, and often a passing grade on a written examination. Employers may require college training, including courses related to the job. The following examples illustrate the range of qualifications for various inspector jobs.

> *Postal inspectors* must have a bachelor's degree and one year's work experience. It is desirable that they have one of several professional certifications, such as that of certified public accountant. They also must pass a background suitability investigation, meet certain health requirements, undergo a drug-screening test, possess a valid state driver's license, and be a U.S. citizen between 21 and 36 years of age when hired.

> *Aviation safety inspectors* working in operations must be pilots with varying certificates, ratings, and numbers of flight hours to their credit. In addition, FAA medical certificates are required. Some also are required to have an FAA flight instructor rating. Maintenance and avionics inspectors must have considerable experience in aviation maintenance and knowledge of industry standards and relevant federal laws. Many aviation

safety inspectors have had flight and maintenance training in the armed forces. No written examination is required.

Applicants for positions as *mine safety and health inspectors* generally must have experience in mine safety, management, or supervision. Some may possess a skill such as that of an electrician (for mine electrical inspectors). Applicants must meet strict medical requirements and be physically able to perform arduous duties efficiently. Many mine safety inspectors are former miners.

Applicants for *internal revenue officer* jobs must be U.S. citizens and must have a bachelor's degree or three years of experience in business, legal, financial, or investigative practices.

Park rangers need at least two years of college with at least 12 credits in science and criminal justice, although some start as part-time, seasonal workers with the U.S. Forest Service. Most positions require a bachelor's degree.

Environmental health inspectors, called *sanitarians* in many states, sometimes must have a bachelor's degree in environmental health or in the physical or biological sciences. In most states, they are licensed by examining boards.

All inspectors and compliance officers are trained in the applicable laws or inspection procedures through some combination of classroom and on-the-job training. In general, people who want to enter this occupation should be responsible and like detailed work. Inspectors and compliance officers should be neat and personable, and be able to communicate well orally and in writing.

Federal government inspectors and compliance officers whose job performance is satisfactory advance up their career ladders to a specified full-performance level. For positions above this level (usually supervisory positions), advancement is competitive, based on agency needs and individual merit.

Advancement opportunities in state and local governments and the private sector are often similar to those in the federal government.

Some civil service specifications, including those for mine inspectors, aviation safety inspectors, and agricultural commodity graders, rate applicants solely on their experience and education. Others require a written examination.

$\mathcal{J}$ob Outlook

Slower than average growth in employment of inspectors and compliance officers is expected through the year 2006, reflecting a balance of continuing public demand for a safe environment and quality products against the desire for smaller government and fewer regulations. Job openings will arise primarily from the need to replace those who transfer to other occupations, retire, or leave the labor force for other reasons. In private industry, employment growth will reflect industry growth, due to continuing self-enforcement of government and company regulations and policies, particularly among franchise operations in various industries.

Employment of inspectors and compliance officers is seldom affected by general economic fluctuations. Federal, state, and local governments—which employ most inspectors—provide workers with considerable job security.

$\mathcal{E}$arnings

The median weekly salary of inspectors and compliance officers, except construction, was about $695 in 1996. The lowest 10 percent earned less than $381; the highest 10 percent earned over $1,215. In the federal government, the annual starting salaries for inspectors varied from $24,200 to $29,600 depending upon the nature of the inspection or compliance activity. Beginning salaries were slightly higher in selected areas where the prevailing local pay level was higher. The following tabulation presents 1997 average salaries for selected inspectors and compliance officers in the federal government in nonsupervisory, supervisory, and managerial positions.

Air safety investigators	$66,110
Highway safety inspectors	64,190
Mine safety and health inspectors	58,000
Railroad safety inspectors	55,910
Internal revenue agents	55,730
Equal employment opportunity officials	54,180
Environmental protection specialists	52,940
Safety and occupational health managers	50,070
Import specialists	49,370
Quality-assurance inspectors	47,020
Customs inspectors	40,020
Securities compliance examiners	39,490
Agricultural commodity graders	39,080
Immigration inspectors	35,010
Consumer safety inspectors	34,360
Food inspectors	32,870
Environmental protection assistants	29,090

Most inspectors and compliance officers work for federal, state, and local governments and in large private firms, all of which generally offer more generous benefits than do smaller firms.

*R*elated Occupations

Inspectors and compliance officers are responsible for seeing that laws and regulations are obeyed. Construction and building inspectors, fire marshals, federal, state, and local law

enforcement professionals, corrections officers, and fish and game wardens also enforce laws and regulations.

Sources of Additional Information

Information on obtaining a job with the federal government may be obtained from the Office of Personnel Management through a telephone-based system. Consult your telephone directory under "U.S. Government" for a local number or call (912) 757-3000 [TDD (912) 744-2299]. The number is not toll-free and charges may result. Information also is available from the OPM's Internet site: www.usajobs.opm.gov.

For information on a career as a specific type of federal inspector or compliance officer, a federal department or agency that employs them may also be contacted directly.

Information about state and local government jobs is available from state civil service commissions, usually located in each state capital, or from local government offices.

Information about jobs in private industry is available from the state Employment Service, which is listed under "Job Service" or "Employment" in the state government section of local telephone directories.

CHAPTER 8

Working as a Paralegal

Significant Points

- Paralegals held about 113,000 jobs throughout the United States in 1996. Private law firms employed the vast majority; most of the remainder worked for the government.
- Employers generally require formal paralegal training obtained through associate or bachelor's degree programs, or certificate programs.
- Paralegals had an average annual salary of $32,900 in 1995. The average annual salary of paralegal specialists who work for the federal government, however, was about $44,400 in 1997.
- Paralegal work is expected to rank among the 20 fastest-growing occupations in the economy as employers rec-

The material in this chapter is adapted from Bureau of Labor Statistics, 1998–1999 *Occupational Outlook Handbook*.

ognize that paralegals perform many legal tasks for lower salaries than lawyers.

*N*ature of the Work

Not all legal work requires a law degree. Lawyers are often assisted in their work by paralegals or legal assistants. Paralegals perform many of the same tasks as lawyers, except for those considered to be the practice of law.

Paralegals work for lawyers. Although the lawyers assume responsibility for the legal work, they often delegate many of their tasks to paralegals. Paralegals are prohibited from setting legal fees, giving legal advice, and presenting cases in court.

Paralegals generally do the preparatory work for lawyers involved in closings, hearings, trials, and corporate meetings. Paralegals investigate the facts of cases, ensuring that all relevant information is uncovered. They conduct legal research to identify the appropriate laws, judicial decisions, legal articles, and other materials that are relevant to assigned cases. After organizing and analyzing the information, paralegals may prepare written reports that attorneys use in determining how cases should be handled. Should attorneys decide to file lawsuits on behalf of clients, paralegals may help prepare the legal arguments, draft pleadings and motions to be filed with the court, obtain affidavits, and assist attorneys during trials. Paralegals also organize and track files of all documents and correspondence important to cases, and make them available to attorneys.

Paralegals may work in all areas of the law, including litigation, bankruptcy, corporate law, criminal law, employee benefits, patent and copyright law, and real estate. They help draft contracts, mortgages, separation agreements, and trust instruments. They may also help prepare tax returns and plan estates. Some paralegals coordinate the activities of other law office employees, and keep the financial records for the office.

Paralegals who work for corporations help attorneys with employee contracts, shareholder agreements, stock option plans, and employee benefit plans. They may help prepare and file annual financial reports, maintain corporate minute books and resolutions, and help secure loans for the corporation. Paralegals may also review government regulations to ensure that the corporation operates within the law.

The duties of paralegals who work in government vary depending on the agency in which they are employed. Generally, paralegals in government analyze legal material for internal use, maintain reference files, conduct research for attorneys, collect and analyze evidence for agency hearings, and prepare informative or explanatory material on the law, agency regulations, and agency policy for general use by the agency and the public.

Paralegals employed in community legal service projects help the poor, the aged, and others in need of legal assistance. They file forms, conduct research, and prepare documents. When authorized by law, they may represent clients at administrative hearings.

Some paralegals, usually those in small and medium-sized law firms, perform a variety of duties that require a general knowledge of the law. For example, they may research judicial decisions on improper police arrests or help prepare a mortgage contract.

Some paralegals employed by large law firms, government agencies, and corporations specialize in one aspect of the law, including real estate, estate planning, family law, labor law, litigation, and corporate law. Within specialties, functions often are broken down further so paralegals may deal with a specific area. For example, paralegals specializing in labor law may deal exclusively with employee benefits.

A growing number of paralegals use computers in their work. Computer software packages and online legal research are increasingly used to search legal literature stored in computer databases and on CD-ROM. The Internet is also used extensively for legal research. In litigation involving many supporting documents, paralegals may use computer databases to organize, index, and retrieve the material. Imaging

software allows paralegals to scan documents directly into a database. Paralegals sometimes use billing programs to track hours billed to clients. They may also use computer software packages to perform tax computations and explore the consequences of possible tax strategies for clients.

Working Conditions

Paralegals do most of their work at desks in offices and law libraries. Occasionally, they travel to gather information and perform other duties.

Paralegals employed by corporations and government usually work a standard 40-hour week. Although most paralegals work year-round, some are temporarily employed during busy times of the year, then released when the workload diminishes. Paralegals who work for law firms sometimes work very long hours when they are under pressure to meet deadlines. Some law firms reward such loyalty with bonuses and additional time off.

Paralegals handle many routine assignments, particularly when they are inexperienced. Paralegals usually assume more responsible and varied tasks as they gain experience. Furthermore, as new laws and judicial interpretations emerge, paralegals are exposed to new legal problems that make their work more interesting and challenging.

Employment

Paralegals held about 113,000 jobs in 1996. Private law firms employed the vast majority; most of the remainder worked for the various levels of government. Within the federal government, the Department of Justice is the largest employer, followed by the Departments of Treasury and Defense, and the Federal Deposit Insurance Corporation. Other employers include state and local governments, publicly funded

legal service projects, banks, real estate development companies, and insurance companies. A small number of paralegals own their own businesses; as freelance legal assistants, they contract their services to attorneys or corporate legal departments.

*T*raining, Other Qualifications, and Advancement

There are several ways to become a paralegal. Employers generally require formal paralegal training obtained through associate or bachelor's degree programs, or certificate programs. Increasingly, employers prefer graduates of four-year paralegal programs, or college graduates who have completed short-term paralegal certificate programs. However, the majority of paralegals hold associate degrees. Some employers prefer to train paralegals on the job, promoting experienced legal secretaries or hiring college graduates with no legal experience. Other entrants have experience in a technical field that is useful to law firms, such as a background in tax preparation for tax and estate practice or nursing or health administration for personal injury practice.

Over 800 formal paralegal training programs are offered by four-year colleges and universities, law schools, community and junior colleges, business schools, and proprietary schools. There are currently 214 programs approved by the American Bar Association (ABA). Although this approval is neither required nor sought by many programs, graduation from an ABA-approved program can enhance one's employment opportunities. The requirements for admission to formal training programs vary widely. Some require some college courses or a bachelor's degree; others accept high school graduates or those with legal experience; and a few schools require standardized tests and personal interviews.

Paralegal programs include two-year associate's degree programs, four-year bachelor's degree programs, or certificate

programs that take only a few months to complete. Many certificate programs only require a high school diploma or GED for admission. Programs typically include general courses on the law and legal research techniques, in addition to courses covering specialized areas of the law, such as real estate, estate planning and probate, litigation, family law, contracts, and criminal law. Many employers prefer applicants with specialized training. Programs increasingly include courses introducing students to the legal applications of computers. Many paralegal training programs include an internship in which students gain practical experience by working for several months in a law office, corporate legal department, or government agency. Experience gained in internships is an asset when seeking a job after graduation.

The quality of paralegal training programs varies; the better programs generally emphasize job placement. Prospective students should examine the experiences of recent graduates of programs in which they are considering enrolling.

Paralegals need not be certified, but the National Association of Legal Assistants has established standards for voluntary certification requiring various combinations of education and experience. Paralegals who meet these standards are eligible to take a two-day examination, given three times each year at several regional testing centers. Those who pass this examination may use the designation *Certified Legal Assistant* (CLA). This designation is a sign of competence in the field and may enhance employment and advancement opportunities. The Paralegal Advanced Competency Exam, established in 1996 and administered through the National Federation of Paralegal Associations, offers professional recognition to paralegals with a bachelor's degree and at least two years of experience. Those who pass this examination may use the designation *Registered Paralegal* (RP).

Paralegals must be able to handle legal problems logically and be able to communicate, both orally and in writing, their findings and opinions to their supervising attorney. They must understand legal terminology and have good research and investigative skills. Familiarity with the operation and applications of computers in legal research and litigation sup-

port is increasingly important. Paralegals must always stay abreast of new developments in the law that affect their area of practice. Paralegals can participate in continuing legal education seminars to maintain their legal knowledge.

Because paralegals often deal with the public, they must be courteous and uphold the high ethical standards of the legal profession. The National Association of Legal Assistants, the National Federation of Paralegal Associations, and a few states have established ethical guidelines paralegals must follow.

Paralegals are usually given more responsibilities and less supervision as they gain more work experience. In large law firms, corporate legal departments, and government agencies, experienced paralegals may supervise other paralegals and clerical staff, and delegate work assigned by the attorneys. Advancement opportunities include promotion to managerial and other law-related positions within the firm or corporate legal department. However, some paralegals find it easier to move to another law firm when seeking increased responsibility or advancement.

ob Outlook

Competition for jobs will continue as the growing number of graduates from paralegal education programs keeps pace with employment growth. Employment of paralegals is expected to grow much faster than average—ranking among the fastest-growing occupations in the economy through the year 2006—as law firms and other employers with legal staffs increasingly hire paralegals to lower the cost, and increase the availability and efficiency, of legal services. While new jobs created by rapid employment growth will create most of the job openings for paralegals in the future, other job openings will arise as people leave the occupation.

Private law firms will continue to be the largest employers of paralegals as a growing population requires additional legal services, especially in areas such as intellectual property,

health care law, international law, elder law, sexual harassment, and the environment. The growth of prepaid legal plans should also contribute to the demand for the services of law firms. A growing array of other organizations, such as corporate legal departments, insurance companies, real estate and title insurance firms, and banks will also hire paralegals.

Job opportunities for paralegals will expand even in the public sector. Community legal service programs—which provide assistance to the poor, aged, minorities, and middle-income families—operate on limited budgets. They will seek to employ additional paralegals in order to minimize expenses and serve the most people. Federal, state, and local government agencies, consumer organizations, and the courts will continue to hire paralegals in increasing numbers.

To a limited extent, paralegal jobs are affected by the business cycle. During recessions, demand declines for some discretionary legal services, such as planning estates, drafting wills, and handling real estate transactions. Corporations are less inclined to initiate litigation when falling sales and profits lead to fiscal belt tightening. As a result, full-time paralegals employed in offices adversely affected by a recession may be laid off or have their work hours reduced. On the other hand, during recessions, corporations and individuals are more likely to face other legal problems, such as bankruptcies, foreclosures, and divorces, that require legal assistance. Paralegals, who provide many of the same legal services at a lower cost, may fare better than lawyers.

*E*arnings

Earnings of paralegals vary greatly. Salaries depend on education, training, experience, the type and size of employer, and the geographic location of the job. Generally, paralegals who work for large law firms or in large metropolitan areas earn more than those who work for smaller firms or in less populated regions.

According to the National Federation of Paralegal Associations, paralegals had an average annual salary of $32,900 in 1995. Starting salaries of paralegals with one year of experience or less averaged $29,300. In addition to a salary, many paralegals received an annual bonus, which averaged about $1,900 in 1995.

The average annual salary of paralegal specialists who work for the federal government was about $44,400 in 1997.

$\mathcal{R}$elated Occupations

Several other occupations call for a specialized understanding of the law and the legal system, but do not require the extensive training of a lawyer. Some of these are abstractors, claim examiners, compliance and enforcement inspectors, occupational safety and health workers, patent agents, police officers, and title examiners.

$\mathcal{S}$ources of Additional Information

General information on a career as a paralegal can be obtained from:

Standing Committee on Legal Assistants
American Bar Association
750 North Lake Shore Drive
Chicago, IL 60611

For information on certification of paralegals, schools that offer training programs in a specific state, and standards and guidelines for paralegals, contact:

National Association of Legal Assistants, Inc.
1516 South Boston St., Suite 200

Tulsa, OK 74119
Homepage: www.nala.org

Information on a career as a paralegal, schools that offer training programs, the Paralegal Advanced Competency Exam, and local paralegal associations can be obtained from:

National Federation of Paralegal Associations
P.O. Box 33108
Kansas City, MO 64114

Information on careers, training programs, and job postings for paralegals is available at the following Internet site: www.paralegals.org.

Information on paralegal training programs, including the pamphlet "How to Choose a Paralegal Education Program," may be obtained from:

American Association for Paralegal Education
P.O. Box 40244
Overland Park, KS 66204

Information on acquiring a job as a paralegal specialist with the federal government may be obtained from the Office of Personnel Management through a telephone-based system. Consult your telephone directory under "U.S. Government" for a local number or call (912) 757-3000 [TDD (912) 744-2299]. That number is not toll-free and charges may result. Information also is available from the OPM's Internet site: www.usajobs.opm.gov.

CHAPTER 9

Working as a Law Enforcement Officer

$\mathcal{S}$ignificant Points

- Police officers, detectives, and special agents held about 704,000 jobs throughout the United States at all levels of government in 1996.
- In larger police departments, where the majority of law enforcement jobs are found, applicants usually must have at least a high school education. Federal agencies, along with an increasing number of state and local police departments, require a college degree.
- In 1996, the median salary of nonsupervisory police officers and detectives was about $34,700 a year, while the highest 10 percent earned over $58,500 a year. Police officers and detectives in supervisory positions had a median salary of about $41,200 a year. Federal agents,

The material in this chapter is adapted from Bureau of Labor Statistics, 1998–1999 *Occupational Outlook Handbook*.

especially at the supervisory level, can earn even higher salaries.

- The number of qualified candidates exceeds the number of job openings in federal law enforcement agencies and in many state, local, and special police departments.

- Opportunities for both employment and advancement will be best in those urban communities whose departments offer relatively low salaries and where the crime rate is relatively high.

Nature of the Work

The safety and well-being of our nation's citizens greatly depends on the police officers, detectives, and special agents responsible for enforcing statutes, laws, and regulations. Duties vary widely by the size and type of organization but in most jurisdictions, whether on or off duty, law enforcement officers are expected to exercise their authority whenever necessary. And, regardless of where they work or what they do, police, detectives, and special agents must spend considerable time writing reports and maintaining records that are needed when legal actions require them to testify in court.

Police officers who work in small communities and rural areas have general law enforcement duties. In the course of a day's work, they may direct traffic at the scene of a fire, investigate a burglary, or give first aid to an accident victim. In large police departments, by contrast, officers usually are assigned to a specific type of duty. Most officers are detailed to patrol a designated area to prevent crime. Patrols generally cover an area such as business districts or outlying residential neighborhoods. Officers may work alone, but in large agencies they usually patrol with a partner. They attempt to become thoroughly familiar with conditions throughout their patrol area and, while on patrol, remain alert for anything unusual. Suspicious circumstances, such as open windows or lights in vacant buildings, as well as hazards to public safety, are noted. They identify, pursue, and arrest suspected crimi-

nals, resolve problems within the community, and enforce traffic laws. Officers are becoming more involved in community policing—building partnerships with the citizens of local neighborhoods and mobilizing the public to help the police fight crime.

Some police officers specialize and become experts in chemical and microscopic analysis, firearms identification, or handwriting and fingerprint identification. Others may work with special units such as mounted and motorcycle patrols, harbor patrols, canine corps, special weapons and tactics or emergency response teams, or task forces formed to combat specific types of crime.

Detectives and *special agents* are plainclothes investigators who gather facts and collect evidence for criminal cases. They conduct interviews, examine records, observe the activities of suspects, and participate in raids or arrests.

Some local departments provide *security officers,* sometimes called *bailiffs,* to maintain order in courtrooms.

Sheriffs and *deputy sheriffs* enforce the law on the county level. In metropolitan areas where there are also regular police departments, the sheriffs department may perform specialized duties such as serving legal documents or operating the jail. A sheriff's duties resemble those of a local or county police chief, but the department is generally on a smaller scale. Most sheriffs departments employ fewer than 25 sworn officers, and many employ fewer than 10.

State police officers (sometimes called *state troopers* or *highway patrol officers*) patrol highways and enforce motor vehicle laws and regulations. They issue traffic citations to motorists who violate the law. At the scene of an accident, they may direct traffic, give first aid, and call for emergency equipment. They also write reports that may be used to determine the cause of the accident. In addition, state police officers may provide services to motorists on the highways, such as calling for road service for drivers with mechanical trouble.

State police also enforce criminal laws. They are frequently called upon to render assistance to officers of other law enforcement agencies. In rural areas that do not have a police force or a local deputy from the sheriffs department, the state

police are the primary law enforcement agency, investigating any crimes that occur, such as burglary or assault.

The federal government maintains a high profile in many areas of law enforcement. *Federal Bureau of Investigation* (FBI) *special agents* are the government's principal investigators, responsible for investigating violations of more than 260 statutes. Agents may conduct surveillance, monitor court-authorized wiretaps, examine business records to investigate white-collar crime, track the interstate movement of stolen property, collect evidence of espionage activities, or participate in sensitive undercover assignments. *Drug Enforcement Administration* (DEA) *special agents* specialize in enforcement of drug laws and regulations. Agents may conduct complex criminal investigations, carry out surveillance of criminals, and infiltrate illicit drug organizations using undercover techniques. *U.S. marshals* and *deputy marshals* provide security for federal courts, including judges, witnesses, and prisoners, and apprehend fugitives. *U.S. Border Patrol special agents* are responsible for protecting more than 8,000 miles of international land and water boundaries. Their primary mission is to detect and prevent the smuggling and unlawful entry of undocumented aliens into the United States and to apprehend those persons found to be in violation of the immigration laws. *Immigration and Naturalization Service* (INS) *agents* facilitate the entry of legal visitors and immigrants to the United States and detain and deport those arriving illegally.

Special agents employed by the U.S. Department of the Treasury work for the Bureau of Alcohol, Tobacco, and Firearms, the U.S. Customs Service, the Internal Revenue Service, and the U.S. Secret Service. *Bureau of Alcohol, Tobacco, and Firearms special agents* investigate violations of federal firearms and explosives laws, as well as federal alcohol and tobacco regulations. *Customs agents* inspect cargo, collect appropriate duties or fees, and intercept contraband while ensuring that all goods entering the United States comply with U.S. laws and regulations. *Internal Revenue Service special agents* collect evidence against individuals and companies that are evading the payment of federal taxes. *U.S. Secret Service special agents* protect the President, Vice President,

and their immediate families; Presidential candidates; ex-Presidents; and foreign dignitaries visiting the United States. Secret Service agents also investigate counterfeiting, the forgery of government checks or bonds, and the fraudulent use of credit cards.

Various other federal agencies employ police and special agents with sworn arrest powers and the authority to carry firearms. These agencies include the U.S. Forest Service under the Department of Agriculture, the National Park Service under the Department of the Interior, and federal *air marshals* under the Department of Transportation. Other police agencies generally evolved from the need for security for the agency's property and personnel. The largest such agency is the General Services Administration's Federal Protective Service, which provides security for federal buildings and property nationwide.

*W*orking Conditions

Police work can be very dangerous and stressful. In addition to the obvious dangers of confrontations with criminals, the need to be constantly alert and ready to deal appropriately with any situation can be very stressful. Police, detectives, and special agents usually work a 40-hour week, but paid overtime work is common. Shift work is necessary because police protection must be provided around the clock. Junior officers frequently must work weekends, holidays, and nights. Police officers, detectives, and special agents are subject to call at any time their services are needed and may work long hours during investigations. All law enforcement officers are required to file reports of their activities, often involving long hours of paperwork. In most jurisdictions, whether on or off duty, officers are expected to be armed and to exercise their arrest authority whenever necessary.

The jobs of some federal agents such as U.S. Secret Service and DEA special agents require extensive travel, often on very short notice. They frequently relocate a number of times over

the course of their careers. Some police, detectives, and special agents with agencies such as the U.S. Border Patrol must work outdoors for long periods in all kinds of weather.

Employment

Police, detectives, and special agents held about 704,000 jobs in 1996. About 63 percent of police detectives and investigators were employed by local governments, primarily in cities with more than 25,000 inhabitants. Some cities have very large police forces, while hundreds of small communities employ fewer than 25 officers each. State police agencies employed about 10 percent of all police, detectives, and investigators; various federal agencies employed the other 27 percent.

Training, Other Qualifications, and Advancement

Civil service regulations govern the appointment of police and detectives in practically all state and large city agencies and in many smaller ones. Candidates must be U.S. citizens, usually at least 20 years of age, and must meet rigorous physical and personal qualifications. Eligibility for appointment generally depends on performance in competitive written examinations as well as on education and experience. Physical examinations often include tests of vision, hearing, strength, and agility.

Because personal characteristics such as honesty, judgment, integrity, and a sense of responsibility are especially important in law enforcement work, candidates are interviewed by senior officers, and their character traits and backgrounds are investigated. In some agencies, candidates are interviewed by a psychiatrist or a psychologist, or are given a

personality test. Most applicants arc subjected to lie detector examinations or drug testing. Some agencies subject sworn personnel to random drug testing as a condition of continuing employment. Although police, detectives, and special agents work independently, they must perform their duties in accordance with the law and departmental rules. They should enjoy working with people and meeting the public.

In larger police departments, where the majority of law enforcement jobs are found, applicants usually must have at least a high school education. Federal agencies generally require a college degree. A few police departments accept applicants as recruits who have less than a high school education, but the number is declining.

The federal agency with the largest number of special agents is the FBI. To be considered for appointment as an FBI special agent, an applicant must either be a graduate of an accredited law school, be a college graduate with a major in accounting, or be a college graduate with either fluency in a foreign language or three years of full-time work experience. All new agents undergo 16 weeks of training at the FBI academy on the U.S. Marine Corps base in Quantico, Virginia.

Applicants for special agent jobs with the U.S. Department of Treasury's Secret Service and the Bureau of Alcohol, Tobacco, and Firearms must have a bachelor's degree or a minimum of three years' work experience that demonstrates the ability to deal effectively with individuals or groups, among other things. Prospective special agents undergo 8 weeks of training at the Federal Law Enforcement Training Center in Glynco, Georgia, and another 8 to 11 weeks of specialized training with their particular agencies.

Applicants for special agent jobs with the U.S. Drug Enforcement Administration (DEA) must have a college degree and either one year of experience conducting criminal investigations, one year of graduate school, or have achieved at least a 2.95 grade point average while in college. DEA special agents undergo 14 weeks of specialized training at the FBI Academy in Quantico, Virginia.

Police departments are encouraging applicants to take postsecondary school training in law enforcement. Many entry-

level applicants to police jobs have completed some formal postsecondary education and a significant number are college graduates. In 1993, the most recent year for which data are available, 12 percent of local police departments required new officer recruits to have at least some college education. Many junior colleges, colleges, and universities offer programs in law enforcement or administration of justice. Other courses helpful in preparing for a career in law enforcement include accounting, finance, electrical engineering or computer science, and foreign languages. Physical education and sports are helpful in developing the courage, competitiveness, stamina, and agility needed for law enforcement work. Knowledge of a foreign language is an asset in many agencies.

Some large cities hire high school graduates who are still in their teens as police cadets or trainees. They do clerical work and attend classes, and can be appointed to the regular force at the conclusion of their training, usually in one to two years, upon reaching the minimum age requirement.

Before their first assignments, officers usually go through a period of training. In state and large local departments, recruits get training in their agency's police academy, often for 12 to 14 weeks. In small agencies, recruits often attend a regional or state academy. Training includes classroom instruction in constitutional law and civil rights, state laws and local ordinances, and accident investigation. Recruits also receive training and supervised experience in patrol, traffic control, use of firearms, self-defense, first aid, and handling emergencies.

Police officers usually become eligible for promotion after a probationary period ranging from six months to three years. In a large department, promotion may enable an officer to become a detective or specialize in one type of police work, such as laboratory analysis of evidence or working with juveniles. Promotions to corporal, sergeant, lieutenant, and captain usually are made according to a candidate's position on a promotion list, as determined by scores on a written examination and on-the-job performance.

Continuing training helps police officers, detectives, and special agents improve their job performance. Through police

department academies, regional centers for public safety employees established by the states, and federal agency training centers, instructors provide annual training in defensive tactics, firearms, use-of-force policies, sensitivity and communications skills, crowd-control techniques, legal developments that affect law enforcement work, and advances in law enforcement equipment. Many agencies pay all or part of the tuition for officers to work toward degrees in criminal justice, police science, administration of justice, or public administration, and pay higher salaries to those who earn such a degree.

Job Outlook

The opportunity for public service through law enforcement work is attractive to many. The job is challenging and involves much personal responsibility. Furthermore, in many agencies, law enforcement officers may retire with a pension after 20 or 25 years of service, allowing them to pursue a second career while still in their forties. Because of relatively attractive salaries and benefits, the number of qualified candidates exceeds the number of job openings in federal law enforcement agencies and in most state, local, and special police departments—resulting in increased hiring standards and selectivity by employers. Competition is expected to remain keen for the higher-paying jobs with state and federal agencies and police departments in more affluent areas. Persons having college training in police science, military experience, or both should have the best opportunities. Opportunities will be best in those urban communities whose departments offer relatively low salaries and where the crime rate is relatively high.

Employment of police officers, detectives, and special agents is expected to increase about as fast as the average for all occupations through the year 2006. A more security-conscious society and concern about drug-related crimes will contribute to the increasing demand for police services. At the

local and state levels, growth is likely to continue as long as crime remains a serious concern. However, employment growth at the federal level will be tempered by continuing budgetary constraints faced by law enforcement agencies. Turnover in police, detective, and special agent positions is among the lowest of all occupations; nevertheless, the need to replace workers who retire, transfer to other occupations, or stop working for other reasons will be the source of most job openings.

The level of government spending determines the level of employment for police officers, detectives, and special agents. The number of job opportunities, therefore, can vary from year to year and from place to place. Layoffs, on the other hand, are rare because retirements enable most staffing cuts to be handled through attrition. Trained law enforcement officers who lose their jobs because of budget cuts usually have little difficulty finding jobs with other agencies.

*E*arnings

In 1996, the median salary of nonsupervisory police officers and detectives was about $34,700 a year. The middle 50 percent earned between about $25,700 and $45,300; the lowest 10 percent were paid less than $19,200, while the highest 10 percent earned over $58,500 a year.

Police officers and detectives in supervisory positions had a median salary of about $41,200 a year in 1996. The middle 50 percent earned between about $29,200 and $38,400; the lowest 10 percent were paid less than $22,500, while the highest 10 percent earned over $64,500 annually.

Sheriffs and other law enforcement officers had a median annual salary of about $26,700 in 1996. The middle 50 percent earned between about $20,300 and $37,800; the lowest 10 percent were paid less than $15,900, while the highest 10 percent earned over $48,400.

Federal law provides special salary rates to federal employees who serve in law enforcement. In addition, federal special

agents receive *availability pay* or *administratively uncontrolled overtime* (AUO) equal to 25 percent of the agent's grade and step, awarded because of the large amount of overtime that these agents are expected to work. For example, in 1996 FBI agents started at a base salary of $33,800 a year, earning $42,250 a year with availability pay. Other Justice and Treasury Department special agents started at about $25,000 or $30,700 a year, earning $31,300 or $38,400 per year including availability pay, depending on their qualifications. Salaries of federal special agents progressed to $55,600 including availability pay, while supervisory agents started at $66,100 including availability pay. Salaries were slightly higher in selected areas where the prevailing local pay level was higher. Because federal agents may be eligible for a special law enforcement benefits package, applicants should ask their recruiter for more information.

Total earnings for local, state, and special police and detectives frequently exceed the stated salary due to payments for overtime, which can be significant. In addition to the common benefits—paid vacation, sick leave, and medical and life insurance—most police and sheriffs departments provide officers with special allowances for uniforms. In addition, because police officers generally are covered by liberal pension plans, many retire at half pay after 20 or 25 years of service.

$\mathcal{R}$elated Occupations

Police, detectives, and special agents maintain law and order. Workers in related occupations include correctional officers, guards, fire marshals, and inspectors.

$\mathcal{S}$ources of Additional Information

Information about entrance requirements may be obtained from federal, state, and local law enforcement agencies. Fur-

ther information about qualifications for employment as an FBI Special Agent is available from the nearest state FBI office; the address and phone number are listed in the local telephone directory.

Further information about qualifications for employment as a DEA Special Agent is available from the nearest DEA office, or call (800) DEA-4288.

Information about career opportunities, qualifications, and training to become a deputy marshal is available from:

United States Marshals Service
Employment and Compensation Division
Field Staffing Branch
600 Army Navy Drive
Arlington, VA 22202

An overview of career opportunities, qualifications, and training for U.S. Secret Service Special Agents is available from:

U.S. Secret Service
Personnel Division, Room 912
1800 G St. NW
Washington, DC 20223

CHAPTER 10

Working as a Private Investigator

$\mathcal{S}$ignificant Points

- Private detectives and investigators held about 58,000 jobs in 1996.
- No formal education requirements exist for applicants, although almost all have experience in other occupations—often in law enforcement or in the military.
- Earnings of private detectives and investigators vary greatly depending on their employers, specialties, and the geographic area in which they work.
- A license is required to work as a private investigator in most areas.
- Employment of private detectives and investigators is expected to grow about as fast as the average for all occupations through the year 2006.

The material in this chapter is adapted from Bureau of Labor Statistics, 1998–1999 *Occupational Outlook Handbook*.

*N*ature of the Work

Private detectives and investigators assist attorneys, businesses, and the public with a variety of problems. Their services include protecting businesses and their employees, customers, and guests from theft, vandalism, and disorder, as well as gathering evidence for trials, tracing debtors, or conducting background investigations. While detectives concentrate on providing protection and investigators specialize in gathering information, many do some of each.

Private detectives' and investigators' duties range from locating missing persons to exposing fraudulent workers' compensation claims. Some specialize in one field, such as finance, where they might use accounting skills to investigate the financial standing of a company or locate funds stolen by an embezzler. Others specialize in locating missing persons, investigating infidelity, or conducting background investigations, including financial profiles and asset searches; others do executive protection and bodyguard work.

Most detectives and investigators are trained to perform physical surveillance, often for long periods of time, in a car or van. They may observe a site, such as the home of a subject, from an inconspicuous location. The surveillance continues using still and video cameras, binoculars, and a citizens' band radio or a car phone, until the desired evidence is obtained. They perform online computer database searches, or work with someone who does. Computers allow detectives and investigators to obtain massive amounts of information in a short period of time from the dozens of online databases containing probate records, motor vehicle registrations, credit reports, association membership lists, and other information.

Private detectives and investigators obtain information by interviewing witnesses and assembling evidence and reports for litigation or criminal trials. They get cases from clients or are assigned to cases by the managers of the firms they work for. Many spend considerable time conducting surveillance, seeking to observe inconsistencies in a subject's behavior. For example, a person who has recently filed a workers' compen-

sation claim stating that an injury has made walking difficult should not be able to jog or mow the lawn. If such behavior is observed, the investigator takes video or still photographs to document the activity and reports back to the supervisor or client.

Some investigations involve verification of facts, such as an individual's place of employment or income. This might involve a phone call or a visit to the workplace. In other investigations, especially in missing persons cases and background checks, the investigator interviews people to gather as much information as possible about an individual.

Legal investigators specialize in cases involving the courts and are normally employed by law firms or lawyers. They frequently assist in preparing criminal defenses, locate witnesses, interview police, gather and review evidence, take photographs, and testify in court. To assist attorneys in the preparation of civil litigation, they interview prospective witnesses, collect information on the parties to the litigation, and search out testimonial, documentary, or physical evidence.

Corporate investigators work for companies other than investigative firms—often large corporations. They conduct internal or external investigations. External investigations may consist of undercover operations aimed at preventing criminal schemes, thefts of company assets, or fraudulent deliveries of products by suppliers. In internal investigations, they may investigate drug use in the workplace, ensure that expense accounts are not being abused, and determine whether employees are stealing merchandise or information.

Detectives and investigators who specialize in finance may be hired to develop confidential financial profiles of individuals or companies who may be parties to large financial transactions, and they often work with investment bankers and accountants. They also may search for assets after fraud or theft, to recover damages awarded by a court.

Private detectives and investigators who work for retail stores or malls are responsible for loss control and asset protection. *Store detectives* safeguard the assets of retail stores by apprehending anyone attempting to steal merchandise or destroy store property. They detect theft by shoplifters, ven-

dor representatives, delivery personnel, and even store employees. Store detectives also conduct periodic inspections of stock areas, dressing rooms, and rest rooms, and sometimes assist in the opening and closing of the store. They may prepare loss prevention and security reports for management and testify in court against persons they apprehend.

*W*orking Conditions

Private detectives and investigators often work irregular hours because of the need to conduct surveillance and contact people who may not be available during normal working hours. Early morning, evening, weekend, and holiday work is common.

Many detectives and investigators spend much time away from their offices conducting interviews or doing surveillance, but some work in their offices most of the day conducting computer searches and making phone calls. Some split their time between office and field work. Those who have their own agencies and employ other investigators may work primarily in an office and have normal business hours.

When working a case away from the office, the environment might range from plush boardrooms to seedy bars. Store and hotel detectives work mostly in the businesses that they protect. Investigators generally work alone, but sometimes work with others during surveillance or when following a subject.

Much of the work detectives and investigators do can be confrontational because the person being observed or interviewed may not want to cooperate. As a result, the job can be stressful and sometimes dangerous. Some detectives and investigators carry handguns. In most cases, a weapon is not necessary because the purpose of the work is generally the gathering of information and not law enforcement or the apprehension of criminals. Owners of investigative agencies have the added stress of having to deal with demanding and sometimes distraught clients.

Employment

Nationwide, private detectives and investigators held about 58,000 jobs in 1996. About 17 percent were self-employed. About 36 percent of wage and salary workers worked for detective agencies, and about 42 percent were employed as store detectives in department or clothing and accessories stores. Others worked for hotels and other lodging places, legal services firms, and in other industries.

Training, Other Qualifications, and Advancement

There are no formal education requirements for most private detective and investigator jobs, although most employers prefer high school graduates; many private detectives have college degrees. Almost all private detectives and investigators have previous experience in other occupations. Some work initially for insurance or collections companies or in the security industry. Many investigators enter the field after serving in military or law enforcement jobs.

Retired law enforcement officers, military investigators, and government agents frequently become private detectives and investigators as a second career. Others enter from such diverse fields as finance, accounting, investigative reporting, insurance, and law. These individuals often can apply their prior work experience in a related investigation specialty. A few enter the occupation directly after graduation from college, generally with majors in such fields as criminal justice or police science.

The majority of the states and the District of Colombia require that private detectives and investigators be licensed by the state or local authorities. Licensing requirements vary widely. Some states have very liberal requirements, or none at all, while others have stringent regulations. For example, the

California Department of Consumer Affairs Bureau of Security and Investigative Services requires 6,000 hours of investigative experience, a background check, and a qualifying score on a written examination. A growing number of states are enacting mandatory training programs for private detectives and investigators. In most states, convicted felons may not be licensed.

In most investigations firms, the screening process for potential employees includes a background check to confirm the applicant's education and work experience, to inquire about the applicant's criminal history, and to interview references and others who know the applicant.

For private detective and investigator jobs, most employers look for individuals with ingenuity who are curious, aggressive, persistent, and assertive. A candidate must not be afraid of being confrontational, should communicate well, and should be able to think on his or her feet. The courts are often the ultimate judge of a properly conducted investigation, so the investigator must be able to present the facts in a manner a jury will believe.

Training in subjects such as criminal justice are helpful to the aspiring private detective or investigator. Most corporate investigators must have a bachelor's degree, preferably in a business-related field. Some corporate investigators have masters of business administration or law degrees, while others are certified public accountants.

Corporate investigators hired by larger companies may receive formal training from their employers on business practices, management structure, and various finance-related topics. Good interviewing and interrogation skills are important and are usually acquired in earlier careers in law enforcement or other fields.

Most investigations firms are small, with little room for advancement. Usually there are no defined ranks or steps, so advancement is in terms of salary and assignment status. Many detectives and investigators work for various investigations firms at the beginning of their careers and after a few years try to start their own firms. Corporate and legal investigators may rise to supervisor or manager of the security or investigations department.

Job Outlook

Employment of private detectives and investigators is expected to grow about as fast as the average for all occupations through the year 2006. In addition, job turnover will create many additional job openings, particularly among wage and salary workers. Nevertheless, competition is expected for the available openings because private detective and investigator careers are attractive to many, and there are many individuals who retire from law enforcement and military careers at a relatively young age who are qualified to enter the field.

Increased demand for private detectives and investigators is expected to be generated by fear of crime, increased litigation, and the need to protect confidential information and property of all kinds. Additional private investigators will be needed by law firms to meet the needs for criminal defense and civil litigation among companies and individuals. Greater corporate financial activity worldwide will increase the demand for investigators to control internal and external financial losses, as well as to find out what competitors are doing and to prevent industrial spying.

Opportunities will be best for entry-level jobs as store detectives or with detective agencies on a part-time basis. Those seeking store detective jobs may find the best opportunities with private guard and security firms since some retail businesses are replacing their own workers with outside contract workers.

Earnings

Earnings of private detectives and investigators vary greatly depending on their employers, specialties, and the geographic area in which they work. According to a study by Abbott, Langer & Associates, security/loss prevention directors and vice presidents earned an average of $67,700 a year

in 1996, investigators about $37,800 a year, and store detectives about $19,100.

Most private investigators bill their clients between $50 and $150 per hour to conduct investigations. Except for those working for large corporations, most private investigators do not receive paid vacation or sick days, health or life insurance, retirement packages, or other benefits. Investigators are usually reimbursed for expenses and generally receive a car allowance.

Most corporate investigators receive health insurance, pension plans, profit-sharing plans, and paid vacation.

Related Occupations

Private detectives and investigators often collect information and protect the property and assets of companies. Others with related concerns include security guards, insurance claims examiners, inspectors, collectors, and law enforcement officers. Investigators who specialize in conducting financial profiles and asset searches do work closely related to that of accountants and financial analysts.

Sources of Additional Information

For information on local licensing requirements, contact your state department of public safety, state division of licensing, or your local or state police headquarters.

CHAPTER 11

Working as a Private Security Officer

$\mathcal{S}$ignificant Points

- Private security personnel held about 955,000 jobs throughout the nation in 1996.
- Many employers of unarmed security personnel do not have any specific educational requirements, although employers generally will not hire applicants who have been convicted of a serious crime.
- Earnings of private security personnel range from about $19,100 per year for guard jobs to an average of $67,700 a year for loss-prevention directors.
- Job opportunities for private security officers are expected to be favorable through the year 2006. High turnover and this occupation's large size rank it among

The material in this chapter is adapted from Bureau of Labor Statistics, 1998–1999 *Occupational Outlook Handbook*.

those providing the greatest number of job openings in
the economy.

*N*ature of the Work

Security officers patrol and inspect property to protect
against fire, theft, vandalism, and illegal entry. Their duties
vary with the size, type, and location of their employers. (Correctional officers—security personnel who work in prisons
and other correctional institutions—and law enforcement
officers are discussed separately in this guide.)

In office buildings, banks, hospitals, and department
stores, guards protect people, records, merchandise, money,
and equipment. In department stores, they often work with
undercover detectives to watch for theft by customers or store
employees.

At air, sea, and rail terminals and other transportation facilities, private security personnel protect people, merchandise
being shipped, property, and equipment. They screen passengers and visitors for weapons, explosives, and other contraband, ensure that nothing is stolen while being loaded or
unloaded, and watch for fires and prowlers. They may direct
traffic.

Security officers who work in public buildings, such as
museums or art galleries, protect paintings and exhibits by
inspecting the people and packages entering and leaving the
building. They answer routine questions from visitors and
sometimes guide tours.

In factories, laboratories, government buildings, data processing centers, and military bases in which valuable property
or information—such as information on new products, computer codes, or defense secrets—must be protected, private
security personnel check the credentials of persons and vehicles entering and leaving the premises. University, park, or
recreation guards perform similar duties and also may issue
parking permits and direct traffic. Golf course patrollers pre-

vent unauthorized persons from using the facilities and help keep play running smoothly.

At social affairs, sports events, conventions, and other public gatherings, private security personnel provide information, assist in crowd control, and watch for persons who may cause trouble. Some guards patrol places of entertainment, such as nightclubs, to preserve order among customers and to protect property.

Armored car guards protect money and valuables during transit. Bodyguards protect individuals from bodily injury, kidnapping, or invasion of privacy.

In a large organization, a security officer is often in charge of the guard force; in a small organization, a single worker may be responsible for all security measures. Patrolling is usually done on foot, but if the property is large, private security personnel may make their rounds by car or motor scooter. As more businesses purchase advanced electronic security systems to protect their property, more guards are being assigned to stations where they monitor perimeter security, environmental functions, communications, and other systems. In many cases, these guards maintain radio contact with other guards patrolling on foot or in motor vehicles. Some private security personnel use computers to store information on matters relevant to security—for example, visitors or suspicious occurrences—during their hours on duty.

As they make their rounds, security personnel check all doors and windows, see that no unauthorized persons remain after working hours, and ensure that fire extinguishers, alarms, sprinkler systems, furnaces, and various electrical and plumbing systems are working properly.

Private security personnel who carry weapons must be licensed by the appropriate government authority, and some receive further certification as special police officers, which allows them to make limited types of arrests while on duty. Unarmed security personnel may carry a flashlight, a whistle, a two-way radio, and a watch clock—a device that indicates the time at which they reach various checkpoints.

Working Conditions

Most security personnel spend considerable time on their feet patrolling buildings, industrial plants, and grounds. Indoors, they may be stationed at guard desks to monitor electronic security and surveillance devices, or to check the credentials of persons entering or leaving the premises. They also may be stationed at gates, or may patrol grounds in all weather.

Because some guards work alone, especially at night, there may be no one nearby to help if an accident or injury occurs. Many security personnel use portable radios or telephones that allow them to be in constant contact with a central station outside the guarded area. If they fail to transmit an expected signal, the central station investigates. Guard work is usually routine, but guards must be constantly alert for threats to themselves and to the property they are protecting. Private security personnel who work during the day may have a great deal of contact with other employees and members of the public.

Many private security personnel work alone at night; the usual shift lasts eight hours. Some employers have three shifts, and guards rotate to divide daytime, weekend, and holiday work equally. Guards usually eat on the job instead of taking a regular break away from the site.

Employment

Private security personnel held about 955,000 jobs in 1996. Industrial security firms and guard agencies employed 59 percent of all such workers. These organizations provide security services on contract, assigning their guards to buildings and other sites as needed. The remainder were in-house security personnel, employed in many settings including banks, building-management companies, hotels, hospitals, retail stores, restaurants, bars, schools, and government agencies.

Private security jobs are found throughout the country, mostly in metropolitan areas.

*T*raining, Other Qualifications, and Advancement

Most states require that private security personnel be licensed. To be licensed as a guard, individuals must generally be 18 years old, pass a background examination, and complete classroom training in such subjects as property rights, emergency procedures, and detention of suspected criminals.

Many employers of unarmed guards do not have any specific educational requirements. For armed security personnel, employers generally prefer individuals who are high school graduates. Some jobs require a driver's license. For positions as armed security personnel, employers often seek people who have had experience in the military or in law enforcement. Most persons entering guard jobs have prior work experience, although it is usually unrelated. Because of the limited formal training requirements and flexible hours, this occupation attracts some persons seeking a second job.

Applicants are expected to have good character references, no serious police record, good health—especially hearing and vision—and good personal habits such as neatness and dependability. They should be mentally alert, emotionally stable, and physically fit in order to cope with emergencies. Security personnel who have frequent contact with the public should be friendly and personable. Some employers require applicants to take a polygraph examination or a psychological profile. Many employers require applicants and experienced workers to submit to drug-screening tests as a condition of employment.

Candidates for guard jobs in the federal government must have some experience as a guard and pass a written examination in order to be certified by the General Services Administration. Armed forces experience is an asset. For most federal guard positions, applicants must qualify in the use of firearms.

The amount of training private security personnel receive varies. Training requirements are higher for armed guards, because their employers are legally responsible for any use of force. Armed guards receive formal training in areas such as weapons retention and laws covering the use of force.

Many employers give newly hired personnel instruction before they start the job and also provide several weeks of on-the-job training. An increasing number of states are making ongoing training a legal requirement for retention of certification. Security personnel may receive training in protection, public relations, report writing, crisis deterrence, and first aid, as well as specialized training relevant to their particular assignments.

Private security personnel employed at establishments placing a heavy emphasis on security usually receive extensive formal training. For example, guards at nuclear power plants undergo several months of training before being placed on duty under close supervision. They are taught to use firearms, administer first aid, operate alarm systems and electronic security equipment, and spot and deal with security problems. Private security personnel who are authorized to carry firearms may be periodically tested in their use. Some security personnel are likewise periodically tested for health, strength, and endurance.

Although guards in small companies receive periodic salary increases, advancement is limited. However, most large organizations use a military type of ranking that offers the possibility of advancement in position and salary. Guards with talent and some college education may advance to jobs that involve administrative and management duties. Security personnel with management skills may open their own contract security guard agencies.

ℐob Outlook

Job opportunities for persons seeking work as private security personnel are expected to be favorable through the year 2006. High turnover and this occupation's large size rank it among those providing the greatest number of job openings in the economy. Many opportunities are expected for persons seeking full-time employment, as well as for those seeking part-time or second jobs at night or on weekends. However, some competition is expected for higher-paying, high-security positions. Compared to unarmed security guards, armed security personnel and special police enjoy higher earnings and benefits, greater job security, more advancement potential, and are usually given more training and responsibility.

Employment of private security personnel is expected to grow faster than the average for all occupations through the year 2006. Increased concern about crime, vandalism, and terrorism will heighten the need for security in and around homes, plants, stores, offices, and recreation areas. Demand for guards will also grow as private security firms increasingly perform duties—such as monitoring crowds at airports and providing security in courts—formerly handled by government police officers and marshals. Because engaging the services of a security guard firm is easier and less costly than assuming direct responsibility for hiring, training, and managing a security guard force, job growth is expected to be concentrated among contract security guard agencies.

Private security personnel employed by industrial security and guard agencies are occasionally laid off when the firm at which they work does not renew its contract with their agency. Most are able to find employment with other agencies, however, and may continue to work at the same location for the firm that won the contract. Guards employed directly by the firm at which they work are seldom laid off because a plant or factory must still be protected even when economic conditions force it to close temporarily.

*E*arnings

Median annual earnings of private security personnel who worked full time in guard positions in 1996 were about $17,300. The middle 50 percent earned between $10,300 and $25,100; the lowest 10 percent earned less than $10,300, and the highest tenth earned more than $35,600. Guards generally earn slightly more in urban areas.

According to a survey of workplaces in 160 metropolitan areas, guards with the least responsibility and training had median hourly earnings of $6.50 in 1995. The middle half earned between $5.50 and $7.92 an hour. Guards with more specialized training and experience had median hourly earnings of $11.73.

Depending on their experience, newly hired guards in the federal government earned $15,500 or $17,500 a year in 1997. Beginning salaries were slightly higher in selected areas where the prevailing local pay level was higher. Guards employed by the federal government averaged about $22,900 a year in 1997. These workers usually receive overtime pay as well as a wage differential for the second and third shifts.

*R*elated Occupations

Private security personnel protect property, maintain security, and enforce regulations for entry and conduct in the establishments at which they work. Related security and protective service occupations include bailiffs, correctional officers, house or store detectives, and private investigators.

*S*ources of Additional Information

Further information about work opportunities for private security personnel is available from local detective and security firms and the nearest state employment service office.

Information about licensing requirements for private security personnel may be obtained from the state licensing commission or the state police department. In states where local jurisdictions establish licensing requirements, contact a local government authority such as the sheriff, county executive, or city manager.

CHAPTER 12

Career Information on the World Wide Web

Significant Points

- Finding employment online is easier than traveling a long way to investigate local job markets.
- A number of free employment services can be found on the Web—any number of which list jobs in the criminal justice and public safety fields.
- Career advice and resume-posting services enhance the value of the Web for job seekers.

Much of the material in this chapter is adapted from the Criminal Justice Distance Learning Consortium, *The Definitive Guide to Criminal Justice and Criminology on the World Wide Web* (1999). Adapted by permission of Prentice-Hall, Inc., Upper Saddle River, N.J.

Finding Employment Online

Not long ago, finding a job took a lot of legwork. Job seekers had to read newspapers and subscribe to special employment services, and sometimes had to travel considerable distances to investigate local job markets. While applying for a job today is still one of the most daunting experiences facing recent college graduates, the process has been made a lot easier by online job banks and electronic employment services.

The federal government maintains a number of job-listing services on the Web, and uses such sites as recruitment tools. One of the most popular is FedWorld (you can reach the jobs page at www.fedworld.gov/jobs/jobsearch.html). If you visit FedWorld you can also click on a selection that reads "Sign up to get FedWorld Vacancy Announcements via Email." Fill out the form that appears, send it to the Fed-World server, and you will quickly find job announcements appearing in your e-mail box. FedWorld also makes available some shareware software packages containing federal job application forms OF612 and SF171, which many folks use to apply for federal jobs.

Some agencies are now posting job application forms directly on the Web. You can complete these forms online, click the *Submit* button at the end of the form, and apply for a job without ever leaving your chair in front of your computer. An online application form for employment as a U.S. Border Patrol agent, for example, is available on line at www.usajobs.opm.gov/BPA1.HTM.

General Listings

General job-listing services frequently provide up-to-date information on positions that are available now. They are a lot like "Help Wanted" sections in newspapers or trade journals. These sites, however, do not necessarily provide other services to the job seeker beyond simple lists. Some criminal justice

and public-safety-related sites, along with their Uniform
Resource Locators (URLs), follow:

Bob's Cops Employment Page

www.cntn.net/bobs
Information on police jobs.

Corrections Jobs

www.corrections.com/jobs
The Corrections Connection job listing service.

FBI Personnel and Employment Page

www.fbi.gov/employment/employ.htm
Information on hiring, recruitment, salaries, and employment statistics.

FedWorld Jobs

www.fedworld.gov/jobs/jobsearch.html
The Web site contains a series of database files using input
from hundreds of human resources people in the federal
government. The database allows you to search abstracts
of open U.S. federal government jobs, and the database is
updated every Tuesday through Saturday at 9:30 A.M. EST.

Ira Wilsker's Law Enforcement Page

www.ih2000.net/ira/ira.htm
An excellent, information-rich site.

Law Enforcement Careers

www.gate.net/~fcfjobs
A full-service career site for those seeking employment
in the law enforcement field. Law Enforcement Careers
categorizes job information as follows: (1) Federal Law
Enforcement Careers, (2) State Trooper Careers, and (3)
Correctional Officer Careers. The site also provides separate testing guides, including the Federal Law Enforcement Testing Guide, and the State and Local Law
Enforcement Testing Guide.

Police Jobs

www.tap.net/~hyslo/poljobs.htm

Extensive list of police employment sites.

The Police Officers' Internet Directory Jobs Page

www.officer.com/jobs.htm

A very comprehensive listing of current law enforcement jobs. Highly recommended for those seeking law enforcement employment.

Public Safety Recruitment

www.psrjobs.com/lawrecru.htm

Established in 1993 to help you reach your law enforcement career goals. PSR provides information from thousands of paid law enforcement agencies from across the nation.

The U.S. Office of Personnel Management

www.usajobs.opm.gov

The U.S. Office of Personnel Management runs a *huge* jobs Web site at this address. All kinds of jobs are listed, but a search feature makes it possible to easily find jobs in the criminal justice area.

State Job Listings

This listing of state-level job opportunities in the criminal justice field is not meant to be comprehensive. The list, however, provides a representative sample of state careers resources.

CALIFORNIA

Criminal Justice Employment Opportunities in California

http://robles.callutheran.edu/scj/employ.html

Berkeley Police Department
www.ci.berkeley.ca.us/bpd/join.html

Los Angeles Police Department
www.cityofla.org/PER/polrecru.htm

Sacramento Police Department
www.sacpd.org/emp_inf.html

FLORIDA

**Florida Department of Environmental Protection
Employment Information**
www.dep.state.fl.us/law/bos/jobs/default.htm

MARYLAND

Baltimore County
www.access.digex.net:80/~issd/career.html

TENNESSEE

Nashville Police
www.nashville.org/pl/job_opportunities.html

WASHINGTON

Spokane Police Department
www.ior.com/~spd/employ.html

Membership Sites

At membership sites, some services are free, but you may have
to first register online, or join the sponsoring association, to
gain full access to these sites. Here's a brief list of such sites:

National Directory of Emergency Services

www1.policejobs.com/ndes/phome.html

Your up-to-the-minute source for police department employment opportunities.

The Public Safety Executive Association (PSEA)

www.policechief.com default.cfm

A membership site that helps members beginning careers in the field of public safety.

General Employment Services on the Web

A number of employment sites on the Web go beyond a mere listing of available jobs. They offer general jobs information, frequently including lots of links to potential employers. We call these sites *general employment services.* A number of them are listed following:

Career Magazine

www.careermag.com

A comprehensive resource designed to meet the individual needs of networked job seekers.

CareerNet

www.careers.org

A listing of over 11,000 links to jobs, employers, and business, education, and career service professionals, and over 6,000 links to employment-related resources.

CareerSite

www.careersite.com

A comprehensive list for job seekers and employers.

CareerWeb

www.cweb.com

A free place to store your resume online. Uses a job-matching function to track your targeted job preferences with e-mail notification.

JobTrak

www.jobtrak.com

A job-listing service that partners with hundreds of college and university career centers. It is used by over 200,000 employers.

Career Advice and Resume-Posting Services

A relatively new idea in seeking criminal justice and public safety jobs exists in the form of sites that help you prepare a resume, advise you on how to submit it to agencies that are currently hiring, or list your resume and credentials online for potential employers to see. You may want to consider posting your own resume online and then directing potential employers to it. Doing so can demonstrate your technical and computer prowess. Sites providing criminal justice career services, including help with resume construction, are listed following:

Career Shop

www.careershop.com

Dr. Carlie's AdviseNet

www.smsu.edu/soc/advnet/advnet.htm

A new concept in online advice for criminal justice students. Provides users with advice on where the field is going, where to find jobs (including many job search

engines) and much more useful information for students at *any* university. The site is maintained by Dr. Mike Carlie of Southwest Missouri State University.

IntelliMatch

www.intellimatch.com

Matches your resume with the needs of prospective employers.

Police Careers

www.policecareers.com

A professional police resume and career-service company.

The MonsterBoard

www.monster.com

Job
Information
Sources
by State

This guide provides jobs information for the nation as a whole. For help in locating state or local-area labor market information, you may wish to contact the following agencies, which are listed here by state.

ALABAMA

Alabama Occupational Information
Coordinating Committee
Alabama Center for Commerce, Room 424
401 Adams Ave.
P.O. Box 5690
Montgomery, AL 36103-5690
Phone: (334) 242-2990

Department of Industrial Relations
649 Monroe St., Room 422
Montgomery, AL 36130
Phone: (334) 242-8859

ALASKA

Alaska Department of Labor
P.O. Box 25501
Juneau, AK 99802-5501
Phone: (907) 465-4500

Alaska Occupational Information
Coordinating Committee
P.O. Box 25501
Juneau, AK 99802-5501
Phone: (907) 465-4518

ARIZONA

Arizona State Occupational Information
Coordinating Council
P.O. Box 6123
Site Code 897J
1789 West Jefferson St., First Floor North
Phoenix, AZ 85005-6123
Phone: (602) 542-3871

Department of Economic Security
P.O. Box 6123
Site Code 733A
Phoenix, AZ 85005
Phone: (602) 542-3871

ARKANSAS

Employment Security Department
P.O. Box 2981
Little Rock, AR 72203
Phone: (501) 682-3159

Occupational Information Coordinating Council
Employment Security Division
Employment and Training Services
P.O. Box 2981
Little Rock, AR 72203-2981
Phone: (501) 682-3159

CALIFORNIA

California Occupational Information
Coordinating Council
1116 9th St., Lower Level
P.O. Box 944222
Sacramento, CA 94244-2220
Phone: (916) 323-6544

Employment Development Department
7000 Franklin Blvd.
Building 1100, MIC 57
P.O. Box 826880
Sacramento, CA 94280-0001
Phone: (916) 262-2160

COLORADO

Colorado Department of Labor
1515 Arapahoe St.
Tower 2, Suite 400
Denver, CO 80202-2117
Phone: (303) 620-4977

Colorado Occupational Information
Coordinating Council
1515 Arapahoe St.
Tower 2, Level 3, Suite 300
Denver, CO 80202
Phone: (303) 620-4981

CONNECTICUT

Connecticut Labor Department
200 Folly Brook Blvd.
Wethersfield, CT 06109
Phone: (860) 566-2121, (860) 566-7963

DELAWARE

Department of Labor
4425 N. Market St.
Wilmington, DE 19809-0965
Phone: (302) 761-8069

Department of Labor
University Office Plaza
P. O. Box 9965
Wilmington, DE 19809-0965
Phone: (302) 761-8050

DISTRICT OF COLUMBIA

District of Columbia Occupational Information
Coordinating Council
500 C St. NW, Suite 200
Washington, DC 20001-2187
Phone: (202) 724-7205

Department of Employment Services
500 C St. NW, Room 201
Washington, DC 20001
Phone: (202) 724-7214

FLORIDA

Bureau of Labor Market Information
Department of Labor and Employment Security
2012 Capitol Circle SE
Hartman Building, Suite 200
Tallahassee, FL 32399-2151
Phone: (904) 488-1048

Department of Labor and Employment Security
The Hartman Building, Suite 200
2012 Capitol Circle SE
Tallahassee, FL 32399
Phone: (904) 488-6037

GEORGIA

Department of Labor
223 Courtland St. NE
Atlanta, GA 30303-1751
Phone: (404) 656-3177

Georgia Occupational Information Coordinating Council
Department of Labor
148 International Blvd.
Sussex Place
Atlanta, GA 30303-1751
Phone: (404) 656-9639

HAWAII

Department of Labor and Industrial Relations
830 Punchbowl St., Room 304
Honolulu, HI 96813
Phone: (808) 586-8999

Hawaii State Occupational Information
Coordinating Council
830 Punchbowl St., Room 315
Honolulu, HI 96813-5080
Phone: (808) 586-8750

IDAHO

Department of Employment
317 Main St.
Boise, ID 83735-0001
Phone: (208) 334-6169

Idaho Occupational Information Coordinating Council
Len B. Jordan Building, Room 301
650 West State St.
P.O. Box 83720
Boise, ID 83720-0095
Phone: (208) 334-3705

*Job Information Sources
by State*

ILLINOIS

Department of Employment Security
401 South State St., 2S
Chicago, IL 60605
Phone: (312) 793-2316

Illinois Occupational Information Coordinating Council
217 East Monroe, Suite 203
Springfield, IL 62706-1147
Phone: (217) 785-0789

INDIANA

Department of Workforce Development
10 North Senate Ave.
Indianapolis, IN 46204-2277
Phone: (317) 233-5724

Indiana Occupational Information
Coordinating Committee
Workforce Development/Technical Education
Indiana Government Center South
10 North Senate Ave., Second Floor
Indianapolis, IN 46204-2277
Phone: (317) 233-5099

IOWA

Department of Workforce Development
1000 East Grand Ave.
Des Moines, IA 50319
Phone: (515) 281-8181

Iowa Workforce Development
200 East Grand Ave.
Des Moines, IA 50319
Phone: (515) 242-5032

KANSAS

Kansas Occupational Information Coordinating
Committee
401 SW Topeka Ave.
Topeka, KS 66603
Phone: (785) 296-3512

Labor Market Information Services
Department of Human Resources
401 SW Topeka Ave.
Topeka, KS 66603-3182
Phone: (785) 296-5058

KENTUCKY

Department of Employment Services
275 East Main St.
Frankfort, KY 40621
Phone: (502) 564-7976

Kentucky Occupational Information
Coordinating Council
500 Mero St., Room 2031
Frankfort, KY 40601
Phone: (502) 564-4258

LOUISIANA

Department of Employment and Training
P.O. Box 94094
Baton Rouge, LA 70804-9094
Phone: (504) 342-3141

Louisiana Occupational Information
Coordinating Committee
P.O. Box 94094
Baton Rouge, LA 70804-9094
Phone: (504) 342-5149

MAINE

Labor Market Information Services
Department of Labor/BES
20 Union St.
Augusta, ME 04330
Phone: (207) 287-2271

Maine Occupational Information
Coordinating Committee
State House Station 71
Augusta, ME 04333
Phone: (207) 624-6200

MARYLAND

Maryland State Occupational Information
Coordinating Council
State Department of Labor, Licensing and Regulation
1100 North Eutaw St., Room 104
Baltimore, MD 21201-2298
Phone: (410) 626-2953

Office of Labor Market Analysis and Information
Department of Labor, Licensing, and Regulations
1100 North Eutaw St., Room 601
Baltimore, MD 21201
Phone: (410) 767-2250

MASSACHUSETTS

Division of Employment and Training
Hurley Building, Fifth Floor
19 Staniford St.
Boston, MA 02114
Phone: (617) 626-6556

Massachusetts Occupational Information
Coordinating Council
Division of Employment Security
Charles F. Hurley Building, Second Floor
Government Center
Boston, MA 02114
Phone: (617) 727-5718

MICHIGAN

Employment Security Commission
7310 Woodward Ave., Room 510
Detroit, MI 48202
Phone: (313) 876-5904

Michigan Occupational Information
Coordinating Committee
Victor Office Center
201 North Washington Square, Fourth Floor
Lansing, MI 48913
Phone: (517) 373-0363

MINNESOTA

Department of Economic Security
390 North Robert St., Fifth Floor
St. Paul, MN 55101
Phone: (612) 296-6546

Minnesota Occupational Information
Coordinating Council
Department of Economic Security
390 North Robert St.
St. Paul, MN 55101
Phone: (612) 296-2072

MISSISSIPPI

Labor Market Information Department
Employment Security Commission
P.O. Box 1699
1520 West Charles St.
Jackson, MS 39215-1699
Phone: (601) 961-7424

Mississippi State Occupational Information
Coordinating Committee
301 West Pearl St.
Jackson, MS 39203-3089
Phone: (601) 949-2240

MISSOURI

Division of Employment Security
421 East Dunkin St.
P.O. Box 59
Jefferson City, MO 65104-0059
Phone: (573) 751-3595

Missouri Occupational Information
Coordinating Committee
400 Dix Road
Jefferson City, MO 65109
Phone: (573) 751-3800

MONTANA

Department of Labor and Industry
P.O. Box 1728
Helena, MT 59624
Phone: (406) 444-2430

Montana Occupational Information
Coordinating Committee
P.O. Box 1728

1301 Lockey St., Second Floor
Helena, MT 59624-1728
Phone: (406) 444-2741

NEBRASKA

Department of Labor
550 South 16th St.
P.O. Box 94600
Lincoln, NE 68509-4600
Phone: (402) 471-9964

Nebraska Occupational Information
Coordinating Committee
P.O. Box 94600
State House Station
Lincoln, NE 68509-4600
Phone: (402) 471-9953

NEVADA

Employment Security Department
500 East 3rd St.
Carson City, NV 89713-0001
Phone: (702) 687-4550

Nevada Occupational Information
Coordinating Committee/DETR
500 East 3rd St.
Carson City, NV 89713
Phone: (702) 687-4550

NEW HAMPSHIRE

Department of Employment Security
32 South Main St.
Concord, NH 03301
Phone: (603) 228-4123

New Hampshire Occupational Information
Coordinating Committee
64 Old Suncook Road
Concord, NH 03301
Phone: (603) 228-3349

NEW JERSEY

Department of Labor, CN056
Trenton, NJ 08625-0056
Phone: (609) 292-2643

New Jersey Occupational Information
Coordinating Committee
Labor Building, Fifth Floor, CN057
Trenton, NJ 08625-0057
Phone: (609) 292-2682

NEW MEXICO

Department of Labor
401 Broadway Blvd. NE
P.O. Box 1928
Albuquerque, NM 87103
Phone: (505) 841-8645

New Mexico Occupational Information
Coordinating Committee
401 Broadway NE
Tiwa Building
P.O. Box 1928
Albuquerque, NM 87103
Phone: (505) 841-8455

NEW YORK

New York State Department of Labor
State Office Building Campus, Room 401
Albany, NY 12240
Phone: (518) 457-6369

New York State Occupational Information
Coordinating Committee
DOL, Research and Statistics Division
State Campus, Building 12, Room 488
Albany, NY 12240
Phone: (518) 457-3806

NORTH CAROLINA

Employment Security Commission
P.O. Box 25903
Raleigh, NC 27611
Phone: (919) 733-2937

North Carolina Occupational Information
Coordinating Committee
700 Wade Avenue
P.O. Box 25903
Raleigh, NC 27611
Phone: (919) 733-6700

NORTH DAKOTA

Job Service North Dakota
P.O. Box 5507
Bismarck, ND 58506-5507
Phone: (701) 328-2868

North Dakota State Occupational Information
Coordinating Committee
1720 Burnt Boat Drive
P.O. Box 5507
Bismarck, ND 58506-5507
Phone: (701) 328-9734

NORTHERN MARIANA ISLANDS

Northern Mariana Islands Occupational Information
Coordinating Committee
P.O. Box 149
Room N-1, Building N
Northern Mariana College
Saipan, CM 96950
Phone: (670) 234-7394

OHIO

Bureau of Employment Services
78–80 Chestnut, Fifth Floor
Columbus, OH 43215
Phone: (614) 752-9494

Ohio Occupational Information
Coordinating Committee
Division of LMI, Ohio Bureau of
Employment Services
145 South Front St.
Columbus, OH 43215
Phone: (614) 466-1109

OKLAHOMA

Employment Security Commission
305 Will Rogers Memorial Office Building
Oklahoma City, OK 73105
Phone: (405) 557-7265

Executive Director
Oklahoma Occupational Information
Coordinating Council
Department of Voc/Tech Education
1500 W. 7th Ave.
Stillwater, OK 74074-4364
Phone: (405) 743-5198

OREGON

Administrator for Research, Tax and Analysis
Oregon Employment Department
875 Union St. NE
Salem, OR 97311
Phone: (503) 378-8656

Oregon Occupational Information
Coordinating Committee
875 Union St. NE
Salem, OR 97311-0101
Phone: (503) 378-5747

PENNSYLVANIA

Director
Bureau of Research and Statistics
300 Capitol Associates Building, Third Floor
901 North Seventh St.
Harrisburg, PA 17120-9969
Phone: (717) 787-3266

Executive Director
Pennsylvania SOICC
Bureau of Research and Statistics
PA Department of Labor and Industry
300 Capitol Associates Building
Harrisburg, PA 17120-0034
Phone: (717) 772-1330

PUERTO RICO

Department of Labor and Human Resources
505 Munoz Rivera Ave., 20th Floor
Hato Rey, PR 00918
Phone: (809) 754-5385

Puerto Rico Occupational Information
Coordinating Committee
P.O. Box 366212
San Juan, PR 00936-6212
Phone: (787) 723-7110

RHODE ISLAND

Department of Employment and Training
101 Friendship St.
Providence, RI 02903-3740
Phone: (401) 277-3730

Rhode Island Occupational Information
Coordinating Committee
101 Friendship St.
Providence, RI 02903
Phone: (401) 272-0830

SOUTH CAROLINA

Labor Market Information
Employment Security Commission
P.O. Box 995
Columbia, SC 29202
Phone: (803) 737-2660

South Carolina Occupational Information
Coordinating Committee
1550 Gadsden St.
P.O. Box 995
Columbia, SC 29202-0995
Phone: (803) 737-2733

SOUTH DAKOTA

Director
Labor Information Center
Department of Labor
P.O. Box 4730
Aberdeen, SD 57402-4730
Phone: (605) 626-2314

South Dakota Occupational Information
Coordinating Council
South Dakota Department of Labor
420 South Roosevelt St.
P.O. Box 4730
Aberdeen, SD 57402-4730
Phone: (605) 626-2314

TENNESSEE

Department of Employment Security
500 James Robertson Pkwy., 11th Floor
Nashville, TN 37245-1000
Phone: (615) 741-2284

Tennessee Occupational Information
Coordinating Committee
500 James Robertson Pkwy., 11th Floor
Volunteer Plaza
Nashville, TN 37245-1600
Phone: (615) 741-6451

TEXAS

Texas Occupational Information
Coordinating Committee
Travis Building, Suite 205
3520 Executive Center Drive
Austin, TX 78731
Phone: (512) 502-3750

Texas Workforce Commission
101 East 15th St., Room 208T
Austin, TX 78778-0001
Phone: (512) 463-2616

UTAH

Labor Market Information
Department of Employment Security
140 East 300 South
P.O. Box 45249
Salt Lake City, UT 84145-0249
Phone: (801) 536-7860

Utah Occupational Information
Coordinating Committee
c/o Utah Department of Employment Security
P.O. Box 45249
140 East 300 South
Salt Lake City, UT 84147
Phone: (801) 536-7806

VERMONT

Policy and Information
Department of Employment and Training
5 Green Mountain Drive
P.O. Box 488
Montpelier, VT 05601-0488
Phone: (802) 828-4153

Vermont Occupational Information Coordinating
Committee
5 Green Mountain Drive
P.O. Box 488
Montpelier, VT 05601-0488
Phone: (802) 229-0311

VIRGINIA

Economic Information Services Division
VA Employment Commission
703 East Main St.
Richmond, VA 23219
Phone: (804) 786-7496

Virginia Occupational Information
Coordinating Committee
Virginia Employment Commission
703 East Main St.
P.O. Box 1358
Richmond, VA 23211
Phone: (804) 786-7496

VIRGIN ISLANDS

Bureau of Labor Statistics
Department of Labor
53A and 54B Kronprindsens Gade
Charlotte Amalie
St. Thomas, VI 00802
Phone: (809) 776-3700

Virgin Islands Occupational Information
Coordinating Committee
P.O. Box 303359
St. Thomas, VI 00803-3359
Phone: (809) 776-3700, extension 2136

WASHINGTON

Labor Market and Economic Analysis
P.O. Box 9046
Olympia, WA 98507-9046
Phone: (360) 438-4804

Washington Occupational Information
Coordinating Committee
c/o Employment Security Department
P.O. Box 9046
Olympia, WA 98507-9046
Phone: (360) 438-4803

WEST VIRGINIA

Labor and Economic Research
JTP/ES Division
Bureau of Employment Programs
112 California Ave.
Charleston, WV 25305-0112
Phone: (304) 558-2660

West Virginia Occupational Information
Coordinating Committee
P.O. Box 487
Institute, WV 25112-0487
Phone: (304) 766-2687

WISCONSIN

Department of Workforce Development
Jobs, Employment, and Training Services Division
201 East Washington Ave.
P.O. Box 7946, Room 221X
Madison, WI 53707-7946
Phone: (608) 266-5843

Wisconsin State Occupational Information
Coordinating Council
Department of Workforce Development, DWE/BW1
201 East Washington Ave.
GEF-1, Room 221X
P.O. Box 7944
Madison, WI 53707-7944
Phone: (608) 267-9611

WYOMING

Research and Planning
Department of Employment
P.O. Box 2760
Casper, WY 82602-2760
Phone: (307) 473-3801

Wyoming Occupational Information
Coordinating Council
P.O. Box 2760
246 South Center St., Second Floor
Casper, WY 82602
Phone: (307) 473-3809

Index